Persuasion Not Manipulation

A Guide to Influencing Others in Everyday Conversations

◄ ❖ ►

Warren D. Benson

TeamBuilders, LLC

ACKNOWLEDGEMENTS

The writing of "Persuasion Not Manipulation: A Guide to Influencing Others in Everyday Conversations" was enriched by the generous support of Dr. Elizabeth Brent, MD, and Mr. Michael Mikolaitis, MA, PMP. The author wishes to express his deep appreciation for their contributions, assistance, and above all, their encouragement during the development of this book.

TABLE OF CONTENTS

"Persuasion is the art of getting people to do what you want them to do because they want to do it."

Dwight D. Eisenhower
U.S. President and General of the Army

ABOUT THIS BOOK

We're born with the ability to influence those around us, from our first cries to our friendships to our romantic partners; from job interviews to giving performance reviews and feedback. All of us are **persuaders**.

We observe and internalize conversational skills and abilities to persuade others as we go throughout our lives, refining and improving upon what works and what doesn't, where they work well and where they don't. We also learn by interacting with others who try, succeed, or fail to persuade us.

Many people, presenters, and organizations have worked diligently to capture and categorize the "magic" that underlies effective persuasion, and to categorize it, perfect it – and then standardize those processes and techniques for use in moving people to or through a decision.

That said, no one likes to feel manipulated, coerced, or handled, and few people like to be "sold to."

But there's a huge difference between manipulation and persuasion.

Persuasion operates out of respect and integrity, and a genuine desire to aid another person or improve their situation – not just simply to reach a goal. It's centered on positively influencing rather than controlling, biasing, or coercing. To persuade effectively, to convince, to motivate, to stimulate another person to action, or even to help someone become "unstuck" in their thinking, the context of the conversation and the relationship between the speaker and listener is very important. Communication should involve sharing information and viewpoints, enabling the listener to maintain the autonomy to make their own decisions. This book focuses on everyday conversations with people in our everyday world, so maintaining a positive relationship is one of your main goals.

A genuine persuasive approach builds and relies upon trust and mutual understanding. It supports and even improves relationships and – most of the time - leads to positive outcomes for both parties. It uses empathy, honesty, a desire to help; it requires ethics and integrity.

I believe that persuasive communication ultimately comes down to heart, passion, and a willingness to help others take a positive step or action - in a way that benefits everyone.

I am confident that by the end of this book you will share this perspective, too.

As you progress through this book, it is **STRONGLY** recommended that you do not read through this entire book in one or two sessions.

Instead, read and digest one approach at a time to allow a short reflection period.

Full references used and consulted in the writing of this book are provided at the end.

"In many ways, effective communication begins with mutual respect, communication that inspires, and encourages others to do their best."

Zig Ziglar
Motivational Speaker and Author

Fostering an atmosphere of respect creates a positive, encouraging environment that empowers and motivates others. This not only facilitates open and honest dialogue, but it also inspires and uplifts the audience, be it a group or an individual, making them more approachable with a message. Persuasive communication is not just about conveying information, it is also about inspiring action.

Chapter 1

THE TWELVE

There are literally dozens (and hundreds of variations) of techniques, approaches, methods, and systems used in a wide range of sales industries that may be found in and studied from hundreds of sales-oriented books and websites. This book focuses on the twelve most-used closing approaches that occur *in routine, everyday conversations*, according to language and psychology experts and my own experience.

Some readers may recognize some of these from their own personal or professional sales interactions. However, it is the intention of this book to demonstrate that these approaches are just as prevalent – and relevant – in day-to-day conversations in the workplace, in the home, between friends, and during interactions in everyday life.

Please note that the following twelve sales closing techniques - *conversational approaches* - are numbered for reference only and are not rank ordered. The actual frequency of these approaches in routine conversations may vary widely based on context, environment, and relationships. In some instances, multiple approaches will be used within a short period of time or even woven together.

As you progress through this book and read about each approach, you'll notice in the various scenarios that there are subtle similarities between several of the twelve approaches and the situations and context in which they're applied.

1. Empathy Close Approach: Creates a connection by aligning with and understanding another person.
2. Assumptive Close Approach: Proceeds as if agreement has already been reached following a guided discussion.
3. Alternative Close Approach: Offers choices or options, rather than on whether to continue the discussion or not.
4. Questions Close Approach: Emphasizes open-ended questions to help the other person verbalize their understanding and acceptance of an idea or proposal.
5. Columbo Close Approach: Uncovers reasons for resistance that are unclear or hidden.

6. <u>Similarity Close Approach</u>: Builds and emphasizes connections, establishing common ground or highlighting a shared experience.
7. <u>Being Inoffensive Close Approach</u>: Maintains positive relations throughout the interaction.
8. <u>Takeaway Close Approach</u>: Generates interest or action when an opportunity may be temporary or short-lived.
9. <u>Ownership Close Approach</u>: Imagines or envisions a future situation or set of circumstances.
10. <u>Ben Franklin Close Approach</u>: Compares choices by separating pros and cons.
11. <u>Sharp Angle Close Approach</u>: Brings stalled conversations to a close and moves toward a decision.
12. <u>Puppy Dog Close Approach</u>: Lets another person try, use, or benefit from something before making a final decision.

For each of these approaches, three scenarios between two people in different situations and contexts will be presented in a conversational format. Read each scenario, then go back and re-read them, noting underlined words and phrases that are most relevant to the close approach being illustrated. Some scenarios will have more underlining than others, and some will have underlining from both individuals.

Following each approach there is a brief discussion illustrating how each approach was applied. In Chapter 14, Putting It All Together, three additional scenarios that combine four approaches within a single conversation are presented and analyzed.

From this point forward, the term "close" will be de-emphasized to reinforce the book's focus on the motivational and conversational aspects of the approaches.

When using any of these approaches, the other individual *ALWAYS* should retain the right to say 'no', challenge or object, or raise concerns.

When this happens, work to overcome the objection or concern (see Chapter 15: Responding to Objections and Concerns).

"People don't care how much you know until they know how much you care."

Theodore Roosevelt
U.S. President and Naturalist

Empathy and genuine concern are important principles in establishing trust and connection – essential ingredients of persuasive communication. Knowledge alone is insufficient to persuade – any receptiveness is enhanced when it's felt that the communicator cares about their interests and well-being.

Chapter 2

THE EMPATHY CLOSE APPROACH

The Empathy Close approach is centered around understanding and aligning with another person. This approach requires genuinely recognizing and addressing the individual's feelings, needs, and concerns, creating a connection that fosters trust and rapport. It is grounded in the psychological principles of understanding and relational communication.

It works by using your ability to understand the other's perspective and by communicating that understanding back to them, projecting a sense of validation and connection. This approach is based on a human need for understanding as well as a desire to be heard and appreciated.

Why it works:

- It builds trust and rapport. By demonstrating a genuine understanding and concern for the other's situation, it fosters a sense of trust and rapport and lays the foundation for more open and meaningful interaction (Rogers, 1951).
- It addresses emotional needs. By tapping into the other's emotional needs, it validates their feelings and makes them feel seen and understood, which is a powerful motivator in decision-making processes (Mayer et al., 1990).
- It enhances communication. This approach promotes effective communication by showing that you truly listen and respond to the other's concerns, which leads to a more personalized and impactful interaction (Rogers, 1951).

The best time to apply it:

- They have expressed emotional concerns or have a strong emotional investment in the decision.
- The interaction is complex and involves understanding nuanced details about their needs or situation.
- You seek to establish a long-term relationship with them, where trust and understanding are important for ongoing interactions.

◆◆◆

This approach is a persuasive method that is based upon the principles of empathy, trust, and effective communication. It addresses another person's emotional and situational needs, encouraging a connection that enables open dialogue and leads to mutually beneficial outcomes.

Empathy Close Approach

Scenario One

> A couple is sitting at the breakfast table discussing the upcoming holiday season. The wife is anxious about disappointing their extended families.
>
> *Read the scenario once, then read through it again noting the <u>underlined</u> areas that are most pertinent to the Empathy Close Approach.*

-ॐ◌ॐ-

Husband (Allen):

Hey, honey, <u>I've noticed you've been feeling pretty stressed</u> lately regarding our holiday plans and which family to visit.

I want you to know that <u>I completely understand</u>, and I don't want you to feel rushed into making a decision.

Wife (Erin):

Thank you for being so understanding.

It's just that I've been torn between wanting to make both families happy and I don't want anyone to feel left out or disappointed.

It's been stressing me out a lot.

Allen:

<u>I hear you, and think your feelings are legit.</u>

I want to make sure we find a solution that feels right for both of us.

Can you tell me more about what's causing the stress and uncertainty?

Erin:

Well, I worry about letting my family down if we don't spend the holiday with them, but I also want to be there with your family.

It's so hard to make a decision because I don't want anyone to feel hurt.

Allen:

I appreciate your honesty, Erin - it's clear to me how much you care about both our families, and I admire your dedication to making sure everyone feels loved and gets their time.

Erin:

Thank you.

That means a lot to me.

I just need a little more time to weigh our options and figure out the best way to handle this.

Allen:

Of course!

Take all the time you need.

We can revisit the discussion when you're ready, and in the meantime, I want you to know that I support whatever decision you ultimately make.

Our happiness is what matters most.

Erin:

Thank you, Allen.

Your willingness to give me more time means the world to me.

I know we'll figure this out together in a way that brings joy to both our families and to us.

-ॐ๏ॐ-

In this conversation, Allen used the Empathy Close Approach to provide a supportive and understanding space for his wife as she navigated the stress of holiday planning with their families. By acknowledging her feelings and the complexity of the situation, he validated Erin's concerns and alleviated the pressure to make an immediate decision. When Allen offered her the time and space she needed to consider the options without rushing, he created an environment of trust and support.

His willingness to revisit the discussion when Erin was ready further strengthened the sense of partnership and shared responsibility in finding a solution.

Empathy Close Approach

Scenario Two

A manager is talking with an employee in his office about a decision she must make. The employee is feeling stressed because of the decision's time sensitivity and its importance.

Read the scenario once, then read through it again noting the <u>underlined</u> areas that are most pertinent to the Empathy Close Approach.

-ᘒᘓ-

Manager (William):

Hi, Linda.

<u>I can sense that you're under a lot of pressure</u> from HR to make a decision about that job candidate for your division.

Employee (Linda):

Hi, William.

Yeah, the pressure has been incessant – they are emailing or calling several times a day.

I want to make the right choice, but I'm worried about making a mistake that could impact the team.

William:

<u>I understand</u>, Linda.

It's a big decision, and <u>I appreciate your concern</u> about the team.

14

What specific worries do you have about this decision?

Linda:

Well, there's the pressure to fill the position quickly because we have a tight timeline, but at the same time I'm concerned about making a rushed decision that might throw off the team dynamics.

William:

I see.

Balancing the need for speed with the need for <u>making the right choice is hard</u>.

Let's look at the potential benefits of each option – making a quick decision and taking the time to ensure a perfect fit.

In other words, how can you address the urgency while still prioritizing the team's long-term success?

Linda:

All good points, William, but I need to take a bit more time and talk to some more members of our team prior to making the final selection.

William:

<u>That sounds like a reasonable plan</u>, Linda.

Take until the end of the week to get more input and come to a decision.

<u>I'll follow up with you Friday – will that be something you can agree to at this point</u>?

I'll run interference with HR if you need me to.

Linda:

Thank you, William.

Your understanding and support mean a lot to me.

೧೯ஒ-

In the scenario, William applied the Empathy Close Approach to support and guide Linda through her decision-making process regarding a job candidate. William began by recognizing and validating Linda's feelings of pressure and concern which reinforced rapport and a trusting atmosphere. He actively listened to her concerns about the urgency to fill the position and the desire to make the right choice, demonstrating understanding and patience.

By suggesting a balanced approach—giving her time to gather input and offering to manage HR's expectations—William reduced the immediate pressure and allowed Linda the space and time to thoroughly evaluate the candidates.

Empathy Close Approach

Scenario Three

> Over lunch, an employee approaches his manager with an idea for a new project he's been thinking about.
>
> *Read the scenario once, then read through it again noting the <u>underlined</u> areas that are most pertinent to the Empathy Close Approach.*

-ᔓᐧᔕ-

Manager (Susan):

Good morning, Liam.

I heard you've been working on a new project idea.

Employee (Liam):

Good morning, Susan.

Yes, <u>I've been brainstorming a project</u> that could potentially improve our customer support efficiency, but it's still in the early stages.

Susan:

I'm intrigued, and I appreciate your initiative.

However, I'm concerned about allocating resources to a project that's not fully developed yet.

<u>Can you provide more details</u> and a clear plan for its execution?

17

Liam:

I understand your concern, Susan.

I've been gathering some initial research and I believe this project could significantly enhance our response times and customer satisfaction.

But I admit that the detailed plan is not yet complete.

Susan:

I see.

It's challenging for me to commit resources to this project at this time.

It's crucial that we prioritize our current projects and maintain our team's focus.

Liam:

I appreciate your perspective, Susan, and I'm determined to refine the project proposal and create a robust plan for execution.

Given some of your concerns, I don't want you to feel pressured to make a decision right now.

How about I send over a better fleshed-out proposal to you later this week and follow up next Wednesday during our regular meeting to see if you can commit to further developing the proposal?

Susan:

Thanks for understanding, Liam.

Yes, please send me some more detailed information, and next Wednesday I'll be able to give you a clear yea or nay.

-⌘⌘-

In the example, Liam used the Empathy Close Approach to navigate the manager's hesitations about a new project idea. It proved effective because it fostered a sense of mutual respect and understanding, ensuring the Manager felt heard and not rushed into a decision, yet still maintained the momentum of Liam's project proposal.

Liam's approach paved the way for a more detailed discussion in the future.

Now that you're familiar with the **Empathy Close Approach**, take a few moments to recall a time when you've used or applied the approach and it was helpful in persuading someone to make a decision or motivating them to take action. You may recognize a time and write about when the approach was used to persuade you, as well.

Briefly describe the situation and outcome below.

_____

_____

_____

_____

_____

_____

Next, imagine a situation in the future where you might use this approach in your professional, social, or personal conversations.

_____

_____

_____

_____

_____

_____

"People may hear your words, but they feel your attitude."

John C. Maxwell
Speaker and Author

Beyond verbal content, it's the speaker's demeanor, sincerity, and passion that truly captivate and influence an audience. Effective persuasion is multi-dimensional because it's not just about what is said, but how it's said and the authenticity behind it. An audience is more likely to be persuaded when they sense a genuine, positive attitude.

Chapter 3

THE ASSUMPTIVE CLOSE APPROACH

The Assumptive Close Approach is where you act under the presumption that the other person has already decided to proceed or they are thinking about making a decision. This method is not about just assuming, but about guiding the interaction toward finalizing the decision. This approach helps the other person agree to what they've already thought through and decided, moving the discussion more quickly along to its anticipated conclusion. It aligns with the psychological theories of commitment and consistency.

This persuasive approach works because of the human desire for consistency in decisions and actions. Once the other person has shown interest or given positive signals toward an idea or proposed course of action, you structure the conversation in a way that assumes the decision has already been made, encouraging the other person in the direction of making a commitment.

Why it works:

- It encourages commitment. By assuming the other person's positive decision, you encourage them to remain consistent with previous actions or indications of interest, which strengthens a commitment toward the decision (Cialdini, 2006).
- It simplifies decision-making. By reducing the complexity of the decision-making process for the other person it shifts the focus from **whether** to go ahead to **how** to go ahead (Fisher, Ury, & Patton, 2011).
- It increases perceived ownership. This approach fosters a sense of ownership and involvement in the decision-making process because the other person recognizes that the decision was theirs all along, and as an extra benefit, it increases their satisfaction and commitment to the decision (Kahneman, 2011).

The best time to apply It:

- They have shown a clear interest or given positive signals about an idea or proposal.

- The discussion is at an advanced stage, they have been thinking about the idea or proposal for some time, or your rapport with them is strong.
- You seek to streamline the decision-making process by reducing indecision or hesitation on their part (Fisher, Ury, & Patton, 2011).

◆◆◆

This approach is a tactful method that uses principles of commitment, consistency, and psychological ownership. It guides the other person toward finalizing a decision to which they're already inclined, making the decision-making process more efficient and agreeable.

Assumptive Close Approach

Scenario One

A wife is sitting with her husband in their living room and wants to propose buying a new sofa.

Read the scenario once, then read through it again noting the <u>underlined</u> areas that are most pertinent to the Assumptive Close Approach.

-·❧·❧-

Wife (Madison):

<u>I've been thinking about redecorating</u> the living room.

<u>What do you think</u> about getting a new sofa?

Husband (Jayden):

What do you have in mind?

Madison:

Well, I found this beautiful sofa online and <u>I think it would really freshen up the space</u>.

It's comfortable, stylish, and it even has a matching coffee table. <u>How about we go check it out</u> this weekend?

Jayden:

Madison…

Our current sofa is still in pretty good shape, and I'm not sure if we need to spend money on a new one right now.

Madison:

I understand your point, Jay.

But think about it this way – a new sofa would not only enhance the look of our living room but also make it more comfortable for both of us.

Plus, we've been talking about updating our furniture for a while now.

This is a fantastic opportunity to do it.

Jayden:

Well, that does sound a bit more reasonable.

Madison:

I like your positivity! [smiles] I knew you'd see the potential.

Let's go visit the furniture store on Saturday and explore our options.

I'm sure we'll find something we'll both love.

Jayden:

Alright, you've convinced me.

We can go check it out on Saturday.

But let's agree to stick to a budget, okay?

Madison:

Of course.

We'll find something within our budget that we both love.

Thanks for being open to the idea!

-⊰⊱-

Madison used the Assumptive Close Approach to guide Jayden toward considering the purchase of a new sofa. By discussing the benefits, she created an environment where the decision to buy seemed natural and beneficial. Her suggestion to visit the furniture store 'this weekend' and the positive framing of the new sofa as a 'fantastic opportunity' to update their furniture implied that the decision had already been made, making it easier for Jayden to go along with the idea.

Madison reduced Jayden's resistance by focusing on the positive aspects of the purchase and assuming that going to the store was the next logical step.

Assumptive Close Approach

Scenario Two

A manager is walking with one of his top employees. He is about to propose a new and more significant role for her he wants to convince her to accept it.

Read the scenario once, then read through it again noting the <u>underlined</u> areas that are most pertinent to the Assumptive Close Approach.

-ॐॐ-

Manager (David):

Hi, Mary.

<u>I wanted to discuss an exciting opportunity with you</u>.

How do you feel about taking on a new role within our department?

<u>The ultimate decision is yours.</u>

Employee (Mary):

Hi, David.

I'm certainly interested in hearing more about it.

What's the new role?

David:

It's a challenging position that involves leading a cross-functional team on a pretty important project.

You've been doing outstanding work in your current role, and I think you have the skills and potential to excel in this new position.

Mary:

That sounds like a significant opportunity, David, and I appreciate your confidence in me.

Can you tell me more about the project and the responsibilities?

David:

The project involves streamlining our processes and improving efficiency.

Your responsibilities would include project planning, team coordination, and ensuring that we meet all deadlines.

With your track record of delivering results, I believe you're the ideal candidate for this role.

Mary:

It does sound challenging!

I'm confident in my abilities, and I'm eager to contribute to the team's success, but are you sure I'm ready?

David:

Your enthusiasm and your strong work ethic make you the perfect fit for this position.

Let's talk about the timeline.

When can I expect you to begin transitioning into the role?

Mary:

Well, I guess I'm ready to start as soon as possible.

Monday?

David:

That's fantastic, Mary.

I appreciate your commitment to taking on this role promptly.

With your skills and dedication, I'm confident you'll make a significant impact on the project and our department as a whole.

Let's get the ball rolling, and I'll work with HR to facilitate the transition smoothly.

Mary:

Thank you, David.

I'll do my best to exceed your expectations.

David:

I have no doubt that you will.

Your enthusiasm and capabilities are exactly what we need for this project.

I'll keep you updated on the next steps, and I'll be here to support you throughout this transition.

Congratulations on your new role!

-𝕖𝕠𝕖-

David effectively used the Assumptive Close Approach to help transition Mary into accepting a new role within the department. He began the conversation by presenting the opportunity in a positive and confident manner, highlighting Mary's qualifications and potential for success in the role, setting the stage for a positive response. Although Mary showed some initial and normal apprehension at taking on a more significant role, throughout the discussion David maintained an assumptive position, focusing on the details of the role and Mary's fit for it.

When David shifted the conversation toward the logistics of the transition ("When can we expect you to begin..."), he further solidified the assumption that Mary would take the role and guided her toward thinking about 'when' rather than 'if'. Mary's responses indicated her interest and readiness, and David's final confirmation and congratulatory remarks reinforced the assumption that the decision had been made.

The Assumptive Close Approach was effective because it created a positive atmosphere without explicitly pressing for a decision.

Assumptive Close Approach

Scenario Three

An employee is meeting with her manager in his office to propose a hybrid work arrangement to her manager.

Read the scenario once, then read through it again noting the __underlined__ areas that are most pertinent to the Assumptive Close Approach.

-ॐॐ-

Manager (Mark):

I understand you want to discuss a potential work-from-home arrangement.

Employee (Jessica):

Yes, and thank you for agreeing to meet.

I've been thinking about this a lot recently.

A hybrid work schedule would provide me with more flexibility and work-life balance.

Mark:

You are an outstanding part of our team, and I'm interested in hearing your proposal.

Let's talk about what you envision for this hybrid schedule.

Jessica:

I was thinking of coming into the office three days a week and working remotely for the other two days.

That way, I can have a mix of face-to-face collaboration and still be able to work from home.

On a predictable and regular schedule, no one should be adversely affected, and I can ensure that my required in-person meetings are booked appropriately.

Of course, I'd be able to come in, if necessary, with enough notice.

Mark:

That sounds like a reasonable and balanced approach, Jessica.

It's important to have a mix that suits your needs and maintains productivity.

Jessica:

I appreciate your willingness to consider this.

How about we formalize the arrangement starting next month?

It will definitely improve my work-life balance and help me manage my personal responsibilities more effectively.

Mark:

This sounds like a pretty good idea.

I'll work with HR to get the necessary paperwork and arrangements in place.

I believe it's important that team members are comfortable and satisfied with their work arrangements.

Jessica:

I appreciate your support, Mark.

I'm confident this will be a positive change, and I'll make sure to keep the team's productivity a top priority.

Thanks again for considering my request.

Mark:

You're welcome, Jessica.

I appreciate your proactive attitude toward finding a solution that works for both you and the company.

Let's make this transition as smooth as possible. I'm looking forward to seeing the benefits it brings.

-ॐॐ-

In this conversation, Jessica applied the Assumptive Close Approach to secure a hybrid work schedule arrangement with her manager. From the outset, Jessica confidently presented her case, detailing the specific days she envisioned working from home and in the office, which implied that she was expecting a positive outcome. Her structured and well-thought-out proposal, coupled with the assurance of maintaining productivity and availability for in-person meetings, framed the request as not only reasonable but anticipated. When she suggested formalizing the arrangement, she assumed his positive response and moved the conversation toward planning and implementation.

This approach reduced potential objections by presenting the arrangement as a natural progression of the conversation rather than as a point for negotiation. Mark's response, acknowledging the balance and reasonableness of the proposal and moving forward with the necessary steps, confirmed that this approach was effective.

Now that you're familiar with the **Assumptive Close Approach**, take a few moments to recall a time when you've used or applied the approach and it was helpful in persuading someone to make a decision or motivating them to take action. You may recognize a time and write about when the approach was used to persuade you, as well.

Briefly describe the situation and outcome below.

_____

_____

_____

_____

_____

_____

_____

Next, imagine a situation in the future where you might use this approach in your professional, social, or personal conversations.

_____

_____

_____

_____

_____

_____

_____

"The art of communication is the language of leadership."

James Humes
Presidential Speechwriter

Persuasive communication shapes perceptions, inspires action, and builds connections. Leaders use this skill to articulate their vision, align their teams, navigate challenges – all the while persuading and motivating their followers. Effective communication drives change, instills confidence, and mobilizes collective efforts toward shared goals.

Chapter 4

THE ALTERNATIVE CLOSE APPROACH

The Alternative Close Approach is where you present a small set of options for the other person to choose from – options that are likely or suitable choices for that person. This method helps guide the person's decision-making process toward selecting one of the offered choices rather than focusing on whether to continue the discussion or not. The psychological foundation of this approach is strongly associated with the paradox of choice and the principle of perceived control.

This approach is effective because it taps into the human tendency to compare options while making decisions. By presenting a controlled set of alternatives, you simplify the decision-making process, effectively narrowing down the scope of decisions to a manageable few. By choosing and agreeing to an option, the other person often has agreed to the larger idea or proposal.

Why it works:

- It reduces being overwhelmed and simplifies decisions. By providing a limited number of options, it reduces the complexity of the decision-making process, preventing a person from feeling overwhelmed by too many choices (Schwartz, 2004).
- It provides a sense of control. People feel more in control of the situation when they are given options to choose from, satisfying their need for autonomy and control in the decision-making process.
- It taps into comparative decision-making. People have a natural tendency to compare options when making decisions. This approach capitalizes on this tendency by presenting the options in such a way that one choice often stands out as the most beneficial (Tversky & Kahneman, 1981).

The best time to apply It:

- They seem overwhelmed by too many possibilities or appear indecisive.

- The idea or proposal being suggested can be distinguished by a few clear and distinctive options.
- You wish to guide them toward making a decision without exerting pressure or overwhelming them with too many choices (Schwartz, 2004).

◆◆◆

This approach is a method that improves the decision-making process by presenting a controlled set of options and minimizing decision fatigue, making it an effective strategy in guiding people toward a commitment.

Alternative Close Approach

Scenario One

A father is sitting with his son and wants to encourage him to complete school homework on a regular schedule.

Read the scenario once, then read through it again noting the <u>underlined</u> areas that are most pertinent to the Alternative Close Approach.

-෧෧ඔ-

Father:

Hey, buddy, <u>I noticed you have some school homework to complete</u>.

<u>When do you think you'll get it done?</u>

Son (Silas):

Hi, Dad.

I'm not really sure, but I was thinking probably later, after I played some video games.

Maybe after dinner?

Father:

That's one option.

But sometimes later doesn't always come, does it?

Silas:

Yeah, sometimes. (embarrassed chuckle)

Father:

What if I gave you a choice?

How about you decide when you want to do your homework during school days.

You can either tackle it right after school to get it out of the way or do it after dinner, as you mentioned.

What works better for you, so you can get everything done you need to and want to?

Silas:

Really, I get to choose?

Well, I guess doing it right after school might be better so that I have more free time later.

Father:

That's a good point.

If you do it right after school, you'll have the whole evening to relax or do whatever you want.

Plus, it leaves your schedule more open.

If you finish your homework early, you can use that time for fun activities.

Silas:

Yeah, that sounds good when you put it that way.

I'll go with doing it right after school then.

Father:

Great choice, Silas.

I'm proud of you!

This way, you'll have more flexibility in your schedule, and it'll help you manage your time better.

If you ever want to change it up or need any help with your homework, just let me know.

Silas:

Thanks, Dad.

I appreciate you giving me a choice and your support.

I'll get started on my homework now and should be done before dinner.

-❧❧-

The Alternative Close Approach was used to guide Silas toward making a responsible decision about completing his homework. By presenting two options for when to do the homework, the father shifted the focus from whether or not to complete the homework to when to complete it. This approach provided a sense of autonomy and control for Silas, making him more receptive and committed.

Because the father offered a choice rather than issuing a directive, he encouraged Silas to take ownership of his decision-making process.

When Silas chose the option of doing homework right after school, the father reinforced the benefits of this choice, emphasizing the increased free time and flexibility it would provide, validating Silas' decision.

Alternative Close Approach

Scenario Two

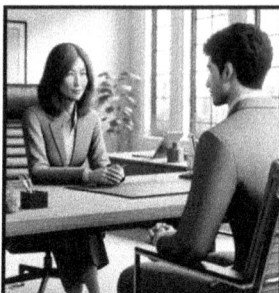

> A manager has called one of her employees into her office to discuss ways to improve his job performance.
>
> ***Read the scenario once, then read through it again noting the <u>underlined</u> areas that are most pertinent to the Alternative Close Approach.***

-⊰०⊱-

Manager (Sarah):

Hi, José.

Thanks for taking the time to meet with me today.

<u>I wanted to have a discussion about your job performance.</u>

Employee (José):

Hi.

I'm always open to feedback and improving my performance.

What's on your mind?

Sarah:

Well, José, overall, you've been doing a great job in your role.

Your attention to detail and dedication to your tasks are commendable.

However, I've noticed that <u>there's some room for improvement in your time management skills</u>, especially when it comes to meeting project deadlines.

José:

I appreciate the feedback.

Yeah, I agree that I could be a little more efficient with managing my time on certain projects.

Sarah:

I'm glad you agree, and I know you have the potential to excel in your job.

To help you improve in this area, <u>I want to discuss two options for you</u>.

José:

Sure, Sarah.

What are they?

Sarah:

<u>Option one</u> is to attend a time management workshop.

It's a half-day training that will provide you with some insights and approaches to better manage your time and meet deadlines more consistently.

<u>Option two</u> is to work closely with a mentor, someone in our department, who excels at time management.

They can provide you with one-on-one guidance.

José:

Both options sound helpful, Sarah.

I appreciate your suggestions.

Sarah:

I'm glad you think so, José.

Which of these options do you think would be more beneficial to you?

Would you prefer to attend the workshop or work with a mentor?

José:

Well, I think working with a mentor would be better for me.

It would give me more personalized guidance and a little bit of accountability.

Sarah:

Excellent choice, José.

I think that's a great decision.

Let's set up a meeting with a mentor who can help you develop your time management skills.

I'm confident that this will contribute to your overall improvement.

José:

Thanks, Sarah.

I appreciate your support and guidance.

I'll work closely with the mentor to get better at managing my time and meeting deadlines.

Sarah:

You're welcome, José.

I have no doubt that you'll make significant progress.

Remember, I'm here to help you when you need it.

Let's schedule that meeting with the mentor and get started on your path to improvement.

José:

I appreciate it, Sarah.

Thanks for helping me with this, and I'll keep you updated on my progress.

Sarah:

That sounds great, José.

I'm looking forward to seeing your growth.

Keep up the good work, and feel free to reach out if you need any further assistance.

-ॐॐ-

Sarah used the Alternative Close Approach to constructively address José's need for improvement while maintaining a supportive environment. By presenting two viable options – a time management workshop or one-on-one mentoring – Sarah provided José with the autonomy to choose the method that best aligned with his personal learning style and needs. This not only ensured that the feedback was received positively but also encouraged José's active participation in his own developmental process. The alternatives offered were both constructive and focused, and allowed José to feel in control of his professional journey.

By making a choice, José committed to a path of improvement, which is likely to be more effective because it's self-chosen. Should José have found neither proposition agreeable, Sarah could have moved on to overcoming an objection (see Chapter 15) to uncover the reason(s) and worked with José toward another mutually satisfactory solution to the issue.

Alternative Close Approach

Scenario Three

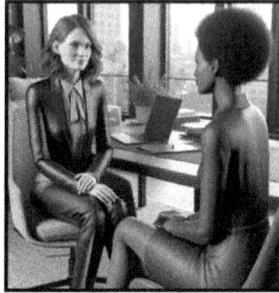

An employee has been called into her manager's office to discuss the time off request she just submitted.

Read the scenario once, then read through it again noting the <u>underlined</u> areas that are most pertinent to the Alternative Close Approach.

-ॐॐ-

Manager (Anita):

Good morning, Lisa.

I see you've submitted a vacation request for next month.

I think we need to discuss it.

Employee (Lisa):

Good morning, Anita.

Yes, <u>I'd like to request some time off</u> to recharge and spend some quality time with my family.

Anita:

I understand the need for a break, Lisa.

Can you tell me more about the dates and the duration of your request?

Lisa:

Sure.

I'm planning to be away from the 15th to the 25th of next month, which is a total of 10 days.

Anita:

That's a lot of consecutive time, Lisa, and it falls during a busy period for our team.

It might impact our project timelines.

Lisa:

I completely understand.

I've thought about it, and <u>I have a couple of alternatives in mind</u>.

<u>One way</u> is to delegate some of my responsibilities to someone who's already said they're willing to cover for me.

<u>Another way</u> is to work extra hours before and after my vacation to ensure that my work doesn't fall behind.

Anita:

Those seem like reasonable alternatives, Lisa.

However, I'm still concerned about any negative impact on the team and project deadlines.

Lisa:

<u>I understand your concern</u>, Anita.

I'm totally committed to maintaining our project timelines and ensuring a smooth workflow.

And <u>to address your concerns</u>, what if I also make myself available for any critical tasks or emergencies that come up during my vacation?

I'll also create a detailed handover document outlining all the ongoing tasks, contacts, and key information for the team to refer to in my absence.

That way, they'll have all the necessary resources to handle any potential issues.

Anita:

That's an interesting proposition, Lisa.

It shows your dedication to the team and our projects.

Let me consider your request, with all that in mind.

Lisa:

Thank you, Anita.

I understand that my vacation request affects the team, and I'm committed to finding a solution that works for everyone.

Please let me know if there's anything else I can do to facilitate this.

I'll stop by tomorrow to see what you've decided.

I'm confident that we can find a solution that works for both the team and my vacation plans.

-ॐॐ-

Lisa used the Alternative Close Approach to address her manager's concerns about her vacation request. She presented alternatives to ensure that her absence would not negatively impact the team's workload or project deadlines. By offering to delegate tasks to a willing colleague, work extra hours before and after the vacation, and make herself available for critical tasks during the vacation, Lisa provided Anita with multiple viable options to choose from.

This approach not only displayed Lisa's commitment to her responsibilities and her team's success, it also provided Anita with the flexibility to choose the solution that best aligned with the team's needs.

The Alternative Close Approach was effective because it shifted the conversation from a potential point of conflict to one of collaborative problem-solving, ensuring that both Lisa's need for a break and the team's project requirements were adequately addressed.

Note: "Let me consider your request" may not sound like a win-win commitment, but by presenting her manager with realistic and viable options, Lisa was able to move Anita from a wary and concerned position to one of consideration. An approval or an opportunity for greater discussion or negotiation was much more likely, rather than a possible denial during a busy time.

Now that you're familiar with the **Alternative Close Approach**, take a few moments to recall a time when you've used or applied the approach and it was helpful in persuading someone to make a decision or motivating them to take action. You may recognize a time and write about when the approach was used to persuade you, as well.

Briefly describe the situation and outcome below.

_____

_____

_____

_____

_____

_____

_____

Next, imagine a situation in the future where you might use this approach in your professional, social, or personal conversations.

_____

_____

_____

_____

_____

_____

_____

"The greatest communication skill is paying value to others."

Denis Waitley
Motivational Speaker and Author

Acknowledging and valuing others is vital to persuasive communication. It requires more than words - it encompasses active listening, empathy, and showing respect toward the other's perspectives and needs. By genuinely valuing others, communicators cultivate trust and rapport and establish a receptive environment for their message. When the other person feels respected and understood, it improves the persuasiveness of the message, because people are more apt to be influenced and take action when they feel seen and are valued.

Chapter 5

THE QUESTIONS CLOSE APPROACH

The Questions Close Approach is characterized by using strategic, open-ended questions aimed at helping the other person verbalize their understanding and acceptance of an idea or proposal. It is also good for figuring out where in the decision-making process the other person is by "checking in." This method is deeply rooted in the principles of active listening and guided discovery, a concept widely discussed in the field of psychology.

This approach operates on the premise that by asking the right questions, you can guide the other person toward articulating their needs and how the idea or proposal fulfills them, effectively helping the other person convince themselves of the value.

Why it works:

- It encourages self-realization. This approach uses a process where the person vocalizes their own needs and how the offer satisfies them, leading to the realization of the idea or proposal's value (Rogers, 1951).
- It enhances engagement. By involving the person in an active dialogue, you keep them engaged and invested in the conversation, making them more receptive to the offer (Rogers, 1951).
- It uses a personalized approach. By tailoring the conversation based on the other person's responses, it ensures that their specific needs and concerns are addressed, which increases the relevance and appeal of your idea or proposal.

The best time to apply it:

- They have not yet fully articulated their needs or seem unaware of how your idea or proposal can benefit them.
- The interaction is more consultative in nature, where they are looking for guidance or expertise.
- You aim to build rapport and a deeper understanding of their needs, ensuring that what you're offering is closely aligned with what they're seeking (Rogers, 1951).

◆◆◆

This approach uses the principles of active listening, guided discovery, and personalized engagement. It effectively guides individuals toward a deeper understanding and acceptance of an idea or proposition.

Questions Close Approach

Scenario One

> While sitting on a porch together, a woman wishes to convince her friend to consider the possibility of changing their regular vacation plans.
>
> *Read the scenario once, then read through it again noting the <u>underlined</u> areas that are most pertinent to the Questions Close Approach.*

-ঙ্কৎ-

Friend One (Zoe):

Amelia, I was thinking about our vacation plans, and I came across this amazing opportunity to travel to the mountains in Colorado this October.

It's such a beautiful location, and the tree colors are supposed to be stunning.

Friend Two (Amelia):

Oh, that does sound nice!

But I'm not sure about changing our vacation destination and date.

The beach in Florida has always been our go-to spot, and we usually go in the summer.

Zoe:

I understand your hesitation, Amelia.

But <u>let me ask you</u>, have you ever experienced the fall foliage in the mountains?

It's a completely different kind of vacation and would be a refreshing change from the beach.

Literally cooler. [laughs]

Amelia:

Well, no, I haven't.

But I worry about the weather.

October might be too chilly for me, Zoe.

Zoe:

Fair point.

<u>But have you considered</u> the cozy cabins and the opportunity to sip hot cocoa by the fireplace while watching the leaves change colors?

It could be such a memorable experience.

Amelia:

I admit that does sound appealing.

But what about the activities we usually enjoy at the beach, like swimming and sunbathing?

Zoe:

I get it, Amelia.

But what if we try something new this time?

The mountains offer activities like hiking, horseback riding, and exploring quaint mountain towns.

<u>Isn't trying new things</u> a part of the adventure of traveling?

Amelia:

You make a good argument. I suppose it could be an exciting change of pace.

Zoe:

That's what I was hoping you'd say, Amelia! I think this trip could be a fantastic opportunity for us to create new memories and explore a different side of vacationing. <u>What do you think</u>?

Amelia:

Alright, Zoe, you've convinced me. Let's go for it – it sounds like an adventure!

-ॐॐॐ-

In this conversation, Zoe used the Questions Close Approach to guide her friend toward considering and eventually accepting a change in their vacation plans. By asking thought-provoking questions, Zoe prompted Amelia to reflect on her preferences and the potential benefits of trying something new.

The questions highlighted unique and appealing aspects of a mountain vacation which were then contrasted with the familiar beach vacation. Each question gently challenged Amelia's initial reluctance and opened her up to the possibility of something new. This approach not only addressed Amelia's concerns (the chilly weather) but also redirected her focus to the positive and novel aspects of the proposed trip.

By involving Amelia in the decision-making process throughout the questions, Zoe ensured that Amelia felt heard and considered, making her more receptive to the idea, eventually leading her to embrace the new vacation plan with enthusiasm.

Questions Close Approach

Scenario Two

During a meeting in the conference room, a manager would like her team to transition to new productivity software and wants to get buy-in and support from her Team Lead.

Read the scenario once, then read through it again noting the <u>underlined</u> areas that are most pertinent to the Questions Close Approach.

-ক্ষ-

Manager (Victoria):

Hi, Liz.

I've been considering the idea of transitioning to a new productivity software system for our team, and I'd like to get your thoughts on it.

Team Lead (Liz):

Well, I'm not entirely convinced about switching to a new system.

Our current one has served us well, and change can be disruptive.

Can you tell me more about why you believe this transition is necessary?

Victoria:

I appreciate your perspective and concern.

The reason I'm proposing this change is that the new software system offers several features that could significantly boost our team's efficiency and productivity.

For example, it streamlines task management, simplifies collaboration, and provides better analytics to track our progress.

Do you see the potential benefits in these improvements?

Liz:

Those benefits do sound promising, Victoria.

However, I'm concerned about the learning curve and the potential disruption to my team during the transition.

We're quite comfortable with the current system.

Victoria:

I understand your concerns.

Transitioning to a new system can be challenging, but I believe the long-term benefits would outweigh the initial inconvenience.

To address the learning curve, we could provide comprehensive training and some additional support to ensure a smooth transition.

What do you think about that?

Liz:

Providing training and support does sound like a good way to mitigate the learning curve, Victoria.

But how do we ensure that the new system aligns with our team's specific needs and workflow?

Victoria:

Great question, Liz.

Before making any decisions, we would conduct a thorough assessment to ensure that the new system can be customized to fit our team's unique workflow and requirements.

This way, we can minimize disruptions and maximize the benefits.

How would you feel about taking part in the assessment process?

Liz:

I appreciate the consideration, Victoria.

If we can ensure that the new system aligns with our workflow and offers proper training, I'm more open to the idea.

Let's explore this further and see if it's a viable option for our team.

-৯৯৫৬-

Victoria employed the Questions Close Approach to engage Liz in a conversation about transitioning to a new productivity software system. By asking open-ended questions, Victoria invited Liz to express her concerns and reservations, enabling a more inclusive and collaborative decision-making process. Each question addressed Liz's apprehensions and steered the discussion toward potential solutions.

The approach not only acknowledged Liz's insights and expertise it also made her an active participant in the evaluation and decision-making process. By carefully listening to Liz's concerns and responding with thoughtful, solution-oriented questions, Victoria effectively transformed resistance into a willingness to consider and explore the proposed change.

Note: When Victoria asked Liz "***What*** do you ***think*** about that?" she could have asked "***How*** do you ***feel*** about that?" Often, the answers and feedback to an emotion-based question (rather than an intellectually based one) will yield different and even more expansive information.

Questions Close Approach

Scenario Three

> Sitting in her manager's office, an employee would like to implement a flexible work schedule for her team.
>
> *Read the scenario once, then read through it again noting the <u>underlined</u> areas that are most pertinent to the Questions Close Approach.*

-ॐॐ-

Direct Report (Amy):

Good morning, Tracy.

I wanted to discuss the idea of moving our team to a flexible work schedule.

Before we delve into the details, <u>may I ask what your main priorities are</u> for the team's performance and productivity?

Manager (Tracy):

Good morning.

My main priorities are ensuring that we meet our project deadlines and maintain high-quality work

I'm concerned about how flexibility might impact our team's ability to collaborate effectively.

I know there are a lot of benefits for staff to have flexible schedules, but I'm not sure in this case it's the best thing for our productivity.

Amy:

That's a valid concern.

To address this, <u>would it help if</u> we implemented core hours where everyone is available for meetings and collaboration, while still allowing for flexibility around those times?

Tracy:

Yes, that sounds like it could work.

But I'm also worried about tracking everyone's progress and ensuring accountability.

Amy:

Understandable.

<u>If we were to use a project management tool</u> that allows us to track progress and set standardized timelines for deliverables for each team member, <u>would that alleviate your concerns</u> about accountability?

Tracy:

It would help.

However, I'm also thinking about how we ensure all team members have access to the support and resources they need while working flexibly.

Amy:

To ensure support and resources are readily available, <u>what if we set up a virtual open-door policy</u> where team members can schedule one-on-one meetings with leads or use dedicated Slack channels for immediate assistance?

Additionally, we could have weekly check-ins to discuss any challenges and resource needs.

<u>Would that approach address your concerns</u>?

Tracy:

Yes, that sounds like a decent plan.

If we can maintain our collaboration, accountability, and support with these measures, I'm open to exploring the flexible work schedule further.

Amy:

Great!

I'll draft a more detailed proposal with these elements and share it with you for feedback.

Thank you for being open to discussing this.

- co-∞-

In the scenario, Amy used the Questions Close Approach to discuss implementing a flexible work schedule with her manager. The use of strategic questions addressed the manager's concerns because each question posed by Amy obtained answers that she could use to construct persuasive arguments for the proposal.

By responding positively and proposing a structured and logical way forward, Amy gently led the conversation toward a positive outcome.

Now that you're familiar with the **Questions Close Approach**, take a few moments to recall a time when you've used or applied the approach and it was helpful in persuading someone to make a decision or motivating them to take action. You may recognize a time and write about when the approach was used to persuade you, as well.

Briefly describe the situation and outcome below.

_____

_____

_____

_____

_____

_____

_____

Next, imagine a situation in the future where you might use this approach in your professional, social, or personal conversations.

_____

_____

_____

_____

_____

_____

_____

"Trust is the highest form of human motivation. It brings out the very best in people. But it takes time and practice."

Stephen R. Covey
Educator and Author

Trust is essential to persuasive communication because it acts as a key motivator and relationship builder. It creates and maintains an environment where people are receptive and open, which enhances the communicator's credibility and the impact of the message. Trust transforms persuasion into a conversation and encourages acceptance and collaboration.

Chapter 6

THE COLUMBO CLOSE APPROACH

The Columbo Close Approach is inspired by the fictional detective Columbo's signature style of inquiry. Using this approach, you revisit a conversation with an afterthought question or statement that prompts the other person to reconsider their decision or view your position from a new perspective. It is effective because of the principles of social courtesy and the Socratic method of asking probing questions to stimulate deeper thinking.

This approach functions by using a twist at the end of a conversation that prompts the other person to think more deeply, often after the other person believes a discussion about the topic has ended. It works on the premise that a well-placed, thoughtful question or statement can shift the other person's perspective or highlight an overlooked benefit of the idea or proposal.

Why it works:

- It encourages deeper engagement. By generating deeper cognitive engagement from the other person by introducing a new angle or consideration, it prompts them to reassess the idea or proposal thoroughly (Paul & Elder, 2006).
- It uses the "element of surprise." The unexpected nature of the question or statement captures their attention and breaks the usual pattern of a conversation, making the interaction more memorable and impactful (Kahneman, 2011).
- It enhances perceived insightfulness. By introducing a thoughtful question or statement, you are perceived as more empathetic and consultative, which enhances the value of the interaction (Schein, 2013).

The best time to apply it:

- They appear to have made up their mind or the conversation seems to be concluding without a decision or commitment.

- You have a meaningful insight or perspective that has not yet been discussed but could significantly impact their decision.
- They value thoughtfulness and would appreciate a deeper, more insightful interaction (Schein, 2013).

◆◆◆

This approach uses elements of surprise, deeper engagement, and insightfulness. It prompts the other person to reconsider an idea or proposal from a new perspective, making it effective in a variety of conversational contexts.

Columbo Close Approach

Scenario One

> At the end of a first date, a man would like to propose a second date, and finds out the woman felt "no chemistry."
>
> *Read the scenario once, then read through it again noting the <u>underlined</u> areas that are most pertinent to the Columbo Close Approach.*

-ॐॐ-

Man (Seth):

I had a great time tonight, and I'd love to see you again.

<u>What do you think about going on a second date</u>?

Woman (Kimberly):

I had a nice time too.

But Seth, I didn't feel a lot of chemistry between us.

Seth:

I appreciate your honesty, Kimberly.

I value chemistry, too. I think we have it, but it takes two, right?

Kimberly:

Yes.

But I did have a good time.

Thank you, and good night.

Seth:

Just out of curiosity, was there anything that killed the chemistry on your end?

I'm wondering if there was anything specific that made you feel that way?

Bad breath?

[smiles]

Kimberly:

No.

[laughs]

It's hard to pinpoint, but I guess one thing that threw me off was when you stepped away and took a phone call during our date.

It made me feel like you weren't fully present and engaged.

Seth:

I can see how that might have given you that impression, and I apologize if it seemed that way.

The call was from my veterinarian about my dog.

He's been sick lately, and he's like family to me.

I had to take the call.

I didn't mean to come across as disengaged.

Kimberly:

Oh!

I see.

I understand how important pets are.

But maybe, next time, you could let your date know in advance if there's a possibility of an urgent call, so they don't feel left out?

Seth:

You're right.

I'll make sure to do that in the future.

And "next time?"

[grins]

If we could have a second date with that understanding, would you be open to it?

Kimberly:

Thank you for explaining, and I appreciate your understanding my initial impressions, as well.

Yes, I'd be open to a second date, as long as I feel I get your attention next time.

[smiles]

Seth:

I'll make our next date more about us and less about phone calls.

I enjoyed getting to know you tonight, and I look forward to a more engaged and focused second date.

-ॐॐॐ-

In the conversation Seth effectively used the Columbo Close Approach to turn a seemingly lost opportunity into a chance for a second date. Seth tactfully used a Columbo-like approach by expressing understanding and then asking a question about what specifically might have negatively affected the chemistry between them. The question opened the door for further dialogue and allowed him to address Kimberly's real concern directly.

After acknowledging the issue and providing a reasonable explanation, Seth reassured Kimberly, who agreed to a second date, showing that a thoughtful question and a willingness to address concerns can lead to a reconsideration of an initial decision, turning a potential 'no' into a 'yes'.

Columbo Close Approach

Scenario Two

Standing in an office doorway and saying farewell, a manager wants to find out about the reasons a valuable team member was resigning.

Read the scenario once, then read through it again noting the underlined areas that are most pertinent to the Columbo Close Approach.

-ᘒᘒᘒ-

Manager (John):

Hi, Marco.

I just heard that you're resigning and I'm genuinely sorry to see you go.

Can you tell me what led to this decision?

Employee (Marco):

Hi, John.

It wasn't an easy decision, but I've received a lucrative offer from another company.

John:

I understand.

Is there something besides pay that may have influenced your decision?

Marco:

No, not really.

But thanks for everything here.

[prepares to leave.]

John:

[shakes Marco's hand.].

Best of luck to you in the future, Marco.

But I can't help but feel there might be more to this.

You've been a valuable member of our team, and all of us thought you were happy here.

I just want to make sure we've done everything we could to keep you here or learn about how we can do things better.

Marco:

Well, honestly John, it wasn't just about the offer.

I've been feeling kind of overlooked and undervalued here recently.

I was taking on more responsibilities without a promotion or even acknowledgement, and doing a good job, but it seems like there hasn't been much recognition or room for growth.

John:

I really appreciate you sharing that, Marco.

I'm genuinely sorry to hear that you've been feeling this way, and I appreciate your honesty.

I want to tell you that your contributions have not gone unnoticed, and I definitely value your dedication to the team.

I'd like to work with you to address these concerns.

What kind of recognition and growth opportunities would you like to see?

Marco:

I'd appreciate more recognition for my efforts and maybe a clearer path for advancement within the company.

I want to know that my hard work is acknowledged and that there's room for career development.

John:

I hear you, Marco.

Let's discuss how we can better recognize your contributions and create a plan for your career growth here.

Would you be open to exploring these options before making your final decision?

Marco:

I appreciate hearing that, John.

I'd be willing to explore those things if there's a genuine commitment to making positive changes.

Let's see what we can come up with together.

-☙❧-

John used the Columbo Close Approach to uncover the deeper reasons behind Marco's decision to resign and to open a dialogue for a potential resolution. His use of open-ended questions and his genuine display of valuing Marco's contributions encouraged Marco to reveal his true feelings about being overlooked and undervalued.

By validating Marco's concerns and expressing a willingness to address them, John effectively created an opportunity for reconsideration and negotiation.

Columbo Close Approach

Scenario Three

Sitting with her supervisor, an employee wants to know why she did not receive a promotion she felt she was qualified for.

Read the scenario once, then read through it again noting the underlined areas that are most pertinent to the Columbo Close Approach.

-ত৯ঙ-

Employee (Alice):

Hi, Mateo, I was hoping we could discuss the recent promotion decision.

I genuinely thought I had a strong chance, but unfortunately it didn't work out.

Can you share some feedback on why I wasn't selected?

Supervisor (Mateo):

Hi, Emily.

I appreciate your interest in your career growth.

The decision was a tough one, and it wasn't just about your qualifications.

We took various factors into consideration.

Alice:

I understand.

I'm eager to learn and improve, so I was wondering if you could help me understand some of those factors better.

Is there anything specific that played a significant role in the decision?

Mateo:

It's not just one thing, Emily.

We considered the entire team's dynamics, the need for diverse skill sets, and some specific project requirements for the promoted role.

Alice:

I see.

I appreciate that, Mateo.

I guess I'll head back to work.

Mateo:

Thank you for coming by Alice.

Please feel free to stop by any time.

Alice:

Mateo, before I go, can you share any specific skills or areas where you think I can improve to be better positioned for future opportunities?

Mateo:

Well, Alice, one area that has come up in discussions is leadership presence and communication.

It's important for roles at this level to demonstrate strong leadership potential.

Alice:

Thank you for sharing that, Mateo - I really value your feedback.

Can you give me a specific example or situation where my communication or leadership may have fallen short so I can work on those aspects?

Mateo:

Well, there were instances during team meetings where your contributions could have been more assertive and confident.

Strengthening your presence in such situations would be helpful.

Alice:

Thank you.

I'll work on being more assertive and confident in team meetings.

Is there anything else that you believe I should focus on for future career growth?

Mateo:

It's glad to hear your commitment, Alice.

In addition to that, consider seeking out opportunities to take the lead on projects and showcase your problem-solving abilities and initiative.

Alice:

I'll definitely take your advice to heart, Mateo.

Thank you for your honesty and for helping me understand how I can improve.

I'm determined to show growth and make a stronger case for future opportunities.

-◈◈-

In the scenario, Alice used the Columbo Close Approach to obtain expanded and specific feedback and guidance from her supervisor. Initially, Mateo provided a general and somewhat generic explanation about the promotion decision-making process. However, Alice tactfully posed additional questions, each leading to more detailed and specific feedback. This approach gently persuaded Mateo to disclose more actionable insights, particularly about Alice's need to enhance her leadership presence, communication skills, and initiative.

By maintaining a polite, inquisitive demeanor and strategically using pointed questions, Alice was able to gather crucial information on how to improve and position herself better for future opportunities, as well as show her commitment to professional growth and receptiveness to feedback.

Now that you're familiar with the **Columbo Close Approach**, take a few moments to recall a time when you've used or applied the approach and it was helpful in persuading someone to make a decision or motivating them to take action. You may recognize a time and write about when the approach was used to persuade you, as well.

Briefly describe the situation and outcome below.

_____

_____

_____

_____

_____

_____

_____

Next, imagine a situation in the future where you might use this approach in your professional, social, or personal conversations.

_____

_____

_____

_____

_____

_____

_____

"Trust is a biological reaction to the belief that someone has our best interest at heart."

Simon Sinek
Motivational Speaker and Author

Successful persuasion is less about the speaker's intent and more about the listener's understanding and emotional engagement – meaning a message shouldn't be just heard, but truly felt and internalized. Effective communication relies heavily upon empathy and clarity, always aiming to bridge any gap between the speaker and an audience. This means trying to create messages that resonate deeply, address the audience's ideals and interests, and elicit the desired response.

Chapter 7

THE SIMILARITY CLOSE APPROACH

The Similarity Close Approach, also known as the "Feel, Felt, Found" Close Approach, is centered around establishing a common ground or shared experience between you and the other person. It operates on the premise that people are more inclined to agree with or accept suggestions from others they perceive as similar to themselves.

"I understand how you *feel*…other people like you have *felt* the same way…but they *found* that…"

This approach involves your identifying and highlighting similarities in background, interests, or challenges with the other person, which creates a sense of rapport and trust. The approach makes the interaction more personal, and the ideas or proposals offered more relatable.

Why it works:

- It builds rapport and trust. Establishing things in common creates a bond between you and the other person, making them more receptive to your suggestions (Cialdini, 2006).
- It increases understanding. They are more likely to believe that someone similar to them understands their needs and situation better, enhancing the validity and applicability of the ideas or proposals.
- It facilitates persuasion through "liking." People are more easily persuaded by individuals they like, and similarity is a key factor in liking. This approach utilizes this principle by helping you to be seen as more likable (and therefor, more persuasive) (Cialdini, 2006).

The best time to apply It:

- They are hesitant or unsure and require a stronger relationship to go ahead.
- You have genuine similarities with them that can be naturally incorporated into the conversation.

- The interaction is in a context where trust and personal rapport are major factors in their decision-making process.

◆◆◆

This approach is based upon the principles of "sameness" and rapport-building. It engenders a sense of trust and understanding that makes ideas and proposals more appealing and persuasive to the other person.

Similarity Close Approach

Scenario One

> During a break in practice, a Music Director wants to provide encouragement to one of his students.
>
> **Read the scenario once, then read through it again noting the <u>underlined</u> areas that are most pertinent to the Similarity Close Approach.**

-❧⊷❦-

Music Director (Mr. Barnes):

Hi there, Grace.

I've noticed that you've been working hard on your performance, but <u>I sense that you might be feeling a bit nervous</u> about it.

Am I off base?

Musician (Grace):

No, Mr. Barnes, you're right.

Lately I've been thinking about how much I stink sometimes, and that I'm really contributing to the group.

Mr. Barnes:

I <u>understand</u>, Grace.

A lot of musicians, including some of the greatest artists, have <u>felt the same way</u> at times.

Heck, that includes me.

We've all had moments when we've felt unsure of ourselves.

Grace:

Really? Even the great musicians? That's hard to believe.

Mr. Barnes:

[laughs]

Even THOSE, not like schoolteachers like me.

[laughs again]

They've <u>all felt that way at some point</u> in their careers.

Myself as well.

But <u>what they found</u> is that these moments of self-doubt are often a sign of personal growth, which leads to a desire to improve.

Grace:

That's an interesting way to look at it, Mr. Barnes.

I never thought of it that way.

Mr. Barnes:

Grace, the most important thing to remember is that you are a talented musician with a unique gift and style.

Your contribution to the group is valuable, and we all appreciate the passion and dedication you bring to our performances.

Grace:

Thank you, Mr. Barnes.

Your words mean a lot to me.

I'll try to focus on improving and not let my insecurities hold me back.

Mr. Barnes:

I like your attitude, Grace.

Keep in mind that everyone's here to support and encourage your talent.

Embrace your uniqueness, and you'll continue to grow as a musician.

-ಎ⊷ఄ-

In this interaction, Mr. Barnes effectively used the Similarity Close Approach to connect with and reassure Grace. By associating Grace's feelings of doubt with the common experiences of other musicians, Mr. Barnes created a sense of shared struggle and understanding, which normalized Grace's emotions and reframed them as a natural part of the artistic journey.

The approach diminished Grace's sense of isolation by showing her that her experiences were not unusual and that a positive outcome was possible. Mr. Barnes' affirming of Grace's talents and contributions to the group provided additional reinforcement and encouragement, motivating her to overcome her insecurities and embrace her role within the group.

Similarity Close Approach

Scenario Two

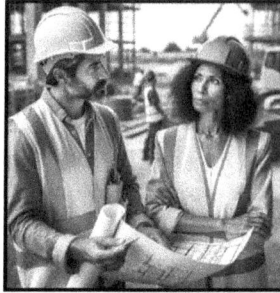

> At a job site, a Project Director needs to share client feedback with one of his Project Managers.
>
> ***Read the scenario once, then read through it again noting the <u>underlined</u> areas that are most pertinent to the Similarity Close Approach.***

-ॐ-

Project Director (Andre):

Good morning, Juliana.

I wanted to discuss some recent feedback we received from a client.

Project Manager (Juliana):

Good morning, Andre.

I'm always open to feedback.

What did the client have to say?

Andre:

Well, Juliana, the client mentioned that they had some concerns about the project's progress and general communication.

They felt that there were moments when they weren't sure about the project's status.

Juliana:

That's disconcerting, Andre, but good to know.

Thanks for telling me.

I'll work on improving communication and ensuring that our clients are well-informed.

If I can't get it up to speed, I can step aside and let a more experienced Project Manager take over.

Andre:

That's not necessary. I understand your concerns as the Project Manager, and just so you know, many Project Managers have faced similar comments and challenges, especially like from this client who felt uncertain about a project's status and progress, for a variety of reasons.

Juliana:

I see, Andre.

It's reassuring to know that I'm not the only one who's faced something like this.

Andre:

Juliana, most of our own team members have been in your shoes.

What they found, and what I'd like to share with you is that clear and proactive communication is key.

Especially the proactive part.

By consistently keeping the client in the loop, addressing their concerns, and providing regular updates, the Project Managers found that the client's confidence in our work increased significantly.

Juliana:

That makes sense, Andre.

I'll make sure to implement this approach and provide better and more frequent communication to our clients moving forward.

Andre:

I'm confident that you'll find this approach to be effective, Juliana.

And your willingness to listen to feedback is appreciated.

Let's work together to ensure our clients have a positive experience working with us.

-ॐ◈-

In this conversation, the Similarity Close Approach was used by the Project Director to both reassure Juliana and guide her toward improving her project management skills. By acknowledging her concerns and then relating them to the common challenges faced by many project managers, including those within their team, the Project Director normalized Juliana's experience.

This approach helped Juliana understand that her situation was not unique but rather a part of the learning and growth process in project management. The Project Director then shared a strategy that other project managers successfully used to overcome similar challenges, alleviating Juliana's apprehension and giving her some guidance and strategies on how to manage the situation.

Similarity Close Approach

Scenario Three

> Two employees are working together in a warehouse discussing the impact of recent changes to their company.
>
> **Read the scenario once, then read through it again noting the <u>underlined</u> areas that are most pertinent to the Similarity Close Approach.**

-ॐॐ-

Employee One (Juan):

Hey, Mei, I've been thinking about the recent changes in the company, and I can't help but worry about potential layoffs.

Employee Two (Mei):

<u>I understand your concern</u>, Juan.

<u>A lot of us have felt the uncertainty lately</u>.

It's a challenging time for sure.

Juan:

Yes, and I'm pretty nervous about it.

Mei:

Have you spoken with any of the other team members who have been through similar situations in the past?

Juan:

No…what would they say?

Mei:

They'd tell you that they found that staying positive, proactive and always working to improve their skills helped them weather the storm.

They also mentioned that networking within the company and keeping lines of communication open with management played a significant role.

Juan:

Thanks, Mei.

I guess staying proactive and adaptable in our roles could be key.

Thanks for sharing that perspective.

And I'll work on staying positive!

[smiles]

Mei:

Of course, Juan.

I think it might help ease some of your concerns.

We're all in this together, and I believe we can navigate the challenges that come our way.

- споδ-

Mei used the Similarity Close Approach to reduce Juan's anxieties about potential layoffs. By Mei's acknowledging his concern, and by mentioning that others were feeling the uncertainty as well, Juan felt less isolated. Mei then expanded on the sense of camaraderie and shared experience by referencing the coping strategies and actions of other team members who had faced similar circumstances. Mei eased Juan's worries and motivated him to adopt a similar approach in navigating the challenges ahead.

Now that you're familiar with the **Similarity Close Approach**, take a few moments to recall a time when you've used or applied the approach and it was helpful in persuading someone to make a decision or motivating them to take action. You may recognize a time and write about when the approach was used to persuade you, as well.

Briefly describe the situation and outcome below.

_____

_____

_____

_____

_____

_____

Next, imagine a situation in the future where you might use this approach in your professional, social, or personal conversations.

_____

_____

_____

_____

_____

_____

_____

"To be persuasive, we must be believable; to be believable we must be credible; to be credible we must be truthful."

Edward R. Murrow
Journalist

Persuasiveness hinges on belief and trust in the communicator. At its core, persuasive communication is not merely about a clever or strategic use of rhetoric or approaches, but about establishing genuine trust through honesty and integrity.

Chapter 8

THE BEING INOFFENSIVE
CLOSE APPROACH

The Being Inoffensive Close Approach is an "other person"-centric approach used when you want to minimize pressure or reduce the potential for confrontation. It operates on the understanding that people are more likely to be receptive and responsive in a low-pressure environment that respects their autonomy and decision-making process.

This approach requires you to carefully present information, allowing the other person to arrive at their conclusions without overt persuasion or pressure. The key is maintaining an atmosphere of respect and understanding, and emphasizing their freedom to choose.

Why it works:

- It respects the other person's autonomy. Recognizing the other person's need for autonomy and self-direction helps maintain a sense of respect and empowerment and makes them more open to interaction (Deci & Ryan, 1985).
- It minimizes resistance. A non-confrontational approach reduces the likelihood of resistance because it eliminates pressure to agree or react defensively (Cialdini, 2006).
- It enables a positive rapport. Engaging in a manner that is perceived as genuine and non-threatening improves rapport and trust between you and the other person (Rogers, 1961).

The best time to apply it:

- They value independence in their decision-making process and may be unreceptive to high-pressure tactics.
- The relationship or potential for future interaction with them is valued, and a respectful, non-intrusive approach is called for.
- You seek to build or maintain a positive, long-term relationship with them, one that emphasizes trust and understanding (Rogers, 1961).

♦♦♦

To summarize, this approach is based upon the principles of respect, autonomy, and non-confrontational communication. It creates and maintains an environment of trust and respect, allowing the other person to feel empowered in the decision-making process.

Being Inoffensive Close Approach

Scenario One

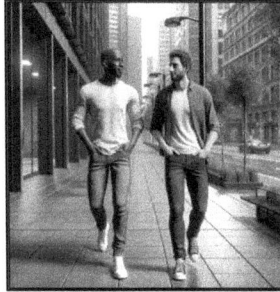

A man brings up his concerns about his friend's health.

Read the scenario once, then read through it again noting the <u>underlined</u> areas that are most pertinent to the Being Inoffensive Close Approach.

-☙❧-

Friend 1 (Sam):

Hey, I've noticed you've been having headaches a lot lately.

<u>How are you feeling?</u>

Friend 2 (James):

Not so great.

I've been trying to manage them with some over-the-counter painkillers, but they don't work so well, and the headaches keep coming back.

Sam:

<u>I'll bet it's tough dealing with that.</u>

Have you thought about seeing a doctor?

James:

Nah.

I'm not sure if it's that serious.

95

It's probably just stress or something.

Dehydration.

[laughs]

Sam:

I get that, but chronic headaches can be a sign of something out of whack.

It's important to rule out any health issues, <u>don't you think</u>?

James:

You're probably right, but I don't want to make a big deal out of it.

Sam:

<u>I totally understand where you're coming from</u>.

Seeing a doctor doesn't necessarily mean it's a big deal.

It's just a precaution to make sure everything is alright.

Plus, <u>it might give you some peace of mind</u>.

James:

Yeah, you're probably right.

I should at least get it checked out.

Sam:

Great!

It's always better to be safe when it comes to your health.

<u>I'll even go with you to the appointment if that makes it easier</u>.

James:

Thanks, that means a lot.

I appreciate your concern and support.

-ॐ৵ও-

The Being Inoffensive Close Approach was employed by Sam to persuade James to consider seeing a doctor. By expressing genuine concern and understanding while emphasizing the importance of health, Sam kept the conversation supportive and non-confrontational. He ensured that James didn't feel judged or pressured, and made the suggestion to see a doctor seem more like friendly advice than nagging. Sam tactfully addressed James' reluctance by acknowledging his concern about overreacting and presented a doctor visit as a simple, precautionary measure. The offer to accompany James to the appointment further reduced any potential anxiety and showed understanding and solidarity.

Being Inoffensive Close Approach

Scenario Two

A manager is in her office opening a discussion with one of her employees about an upcoming workspace redesign.

Read the scenario once, then read through it again noting the <u>underlined</u> areas that are most pertinent to the Being Inoffensive Close Approach.

-෨෧-

HR Manager (Emme):

Good morning, Adam.

I wanted to talk to you about the upcoming move to our new office space.

Programmer (Adam):

Good morning.

Yes, I've heard about it.

I'm pretty concerned about the new layout.

I've always had my own office, and now I'll be in a cubicle?

Emme:

<u>I appreciate your concerns</u>, Adam.

The company's made a decision to optimize our workspace, and it's essential for us to adapt to these changes.

The new layout is designed to foster collaboration and a more open working environment.

Adam:

I see that, but I've always valued my privacy and quiet space in my office.

It's going to be quite an adjustment for me, Emme.

Emme:

I completely understand your wanting to keep your office, and I value your work and dedication to the company.

But I believe that you'll still have a productive and comfortable workspace in the new layout.

Many employees have found that the transition to a more open environment leads to increased collaboration and creativity.

Even better morale.

Adam:

I'm just worried about distractions and the lack of privacy.

What if I need to have a confidential conversation with a colleague or client?

Emme:

Your concerns are valid, and we've considered that.

We'll be establishing private meeting areas and soundproof rooms where you can have confidential discussions without any interruptions.

Adam:

That does help alleviate some of my worries, but I'm still hesitant.

Emme:

I appreciate your honesty, Adam.

I want you to know that your comfort and productivity are important.

We're willing to work with you during this transition to ensure you have everything you need to be successful.

Adam:

Emme, I appreciate your willingness to work with me on this.

I suppose I can give it a try.

Emme:

Thank you, Adam.

Your flexibility and open-mindedness are very appreciated, and I'm optimistic that you'll find the new environment to be a positive change after an adjustment period.

We'll be here to support you throughout the process.

-ॐॐ-

Emme employed the Being Inoffensive Close Approach to address Adam's concerns in a non-confrontational way. She acknowledged and validated Adam's apprehensions while providing reassurance and highlighted the benefits of the new workspace design. By offering concrete solutions like private meeting areas and soundproofed rooms, Emme addressed specific concerns and diminished Adam's resistance.

Emme's assurance of ongoing support during the transition period helped alleviate Adam's anxiety.

Being Inoffensive Close Approach

Scenario Three

A police officer is approaching a motorist who has been pulled over for not stopping at a red light.

Read the scenario once, then read through it again noting the underlined areas that are most pertinent to the Being Inoffensive Close Approach.

-ॐ-

Motorist:

Good evening, Officer. I know I just ran that red light.

Police Officer:

Evening, sir.

Yes, you did.

Running a red light, especially around here, is very dangerous.

May I see your license and registration?

Motorist:

[Hands documents]

Officer, I have no excuse for running the light.

I wasn't paying attention. I know it was dangerous.

Police Officer:

I appreciate your honesty, sir, and cooperation.

I'll be back in a minute with your documents.

Police Officer:

[Returns]

It's important that you admitted you made a mistake and didn't make any excuses.

At first I was going to issue you a citation, but instead I'm going to give you a warning.

Pay more attention on your way home, okay?

Motorist:

Officer, <u>again, I'm really sorry</u>.

<u>And thank you</u>!

I promise to be more alert.

-ॐॐ-

In this conversation, the motorist employed the Being Inoffensive Close Approach to navigate a negative situation with a police officer into a more positive one. By acknowledging the mistake and expressing genuine remorse without making excuses, the motorist established a respectful and cooperative tone. The honest and humble approach defused potential defensiveness from the officer.

The non-confrontational, sincere, and respectful attitude encouraged the officer to consider an alternative consequence.

Now that you're familiar with the **Being Inoffensive Close Approach**, take a few moments to recall a time when you've used or applied the approach and it was helpful in persuading someone to make a decision or motivating them to take action. You may recognize a time and write about when the approach was used to persuade you, as well.

Briefly describe the situation and outcome below.

_____

_____

_____

_____

_____

_____

Next, imagine a situation in the future where you might use this approach in your professional, social, or personal conversations.

_____

_____

_____

_____

_____

_____

_____

"I've learned that people will forget what you said, people will forget what you did, but people will never forget how you made them feel."

Maya Angelou
Poet and Activist

There is an enduring power of emotional impact in persuasive communication. While the content of a message and actions taken may fade in memory, emotional imprints are lasting. The need to connect on an emotional level is important for communicators because persuasion is not just about the clarity of the message or the actions that support it, but also about the ability to evoke feelings that ensure a message is not just heard but felt, acted on, and remembered.

Chapter 9

THE TAKEAWAY CLOSE APPROACH

The Takeaway Close Approach is a conversational tack that is sometimes employed during discussions that are negotiating in nature. It is characterized by reminding the other person that an opportunity might not be available for an extended period or under certain conditions. This method is deeply rooted in psychological principles related to scarcity and loss aversion.

The psychological basis for this approach is well documented in works such as Robert B. Cialdini's "Influence: The Psychology of Persuasion." Cialdini shows how humans are "wired" to place a high value on things that are scarce or at risk of being lost. The Takeaway Close Approach uses this principle by creating a sense of urgency or exclusivity.

Why it works:

- It operates on the Scarcity Principle. When an offer or opportunity is presented as rare or limited, it is perceived as more valuable, which often produces a quicker response from the other person (Cialdini, 2006).
- It touches on Loss Aversion. By tapping into the concept of loss aversion, where individuals prefer avoiding losses over acquiring equivalent gains, it reminds the other person about the potential loss of an opportunity, and the perceived value of the offer increases (Tversky & Kahneman, 1991).
- It encourages decisiveness. By creating a sense of urgency, it helps the other person make a decision swiftly to avoid missing out on the offer or opportunity. This urgency reduces their tendency to procrastinate or defer a decision (Monroe, 2003).

The best time to apply It:

- They appear interested but hesitant, possibly due to indecision or the exploration of other options.
- The offer genuinely has limitations in terms of availability or conditions.

- They value the offer and are likely to be motivated by the potential of losing access to it if they do not act promptly (Cialdini, 2006).

◆◆◆

This approach relies on fundamental psychological principles such as scarcity and loss aversion. It creates a sense of urgency and increases the perceived value of the idea or proposal, prompting the other person to make decisions more quickly.

Takeaway Close Approach

Scenario One

During breakfast at a sidewalk café, one friend makes a comment about beginning an exercise program.

Read the scenario once, then read through it again noting the <u>underlined</u> areas that are most pertinent to the Takeaway Close Approach.

-ॐॐ-

Friend One (Liv):

I've been thinking about starting an exercise routine, you know, to get in better shape and feel healthier.

Friend Two (Dana):

Liv, that's awesome!

Exercise has so many benefits, like improved energy levels and overall well-being.

Liv:

Yeah, but doesn't it take a lot of time and effort to see significant results?

I've heard it can be quite a commitment, and sometimes it's hard to find the motivation.

Dana:

Sometimes it is tough, especially when life gets busy – which is pretty much always.

And there's the thing about finding the type of exercise you enjoy that fits your schedule.

Liv:

Yeah!

It's a lot to consider.

Maybe it's just not the right time for me to start.

Dana:

Liv, I get it…if you're not into it, you're not into it.

It's important to be committed before you begin.

Maybe it's just better for you to focus on other aspects of your health right now…

Liv:

But I really want to give it a shot…

Dana:

I'll tell you what:

why don't you just "give it a shot" like you said?

I'll be a cheerleader for you, and even work out with you from time to time to help you stay on track.

No time like the present, right?

-ଵଵୖ-

Dana used the Takeaway Close Approach to reignite Liv's motivation to start an exercise routine. Initially, Dana empathized with Liv's concerns, even suggesting that it might not be the right time to start, which reduced pressure and made the idea of not pursuing the routine seem reasonable.

The momentary withdrawal or 'takeaway' of the idea played a crucial role because it made the option of exercise more attractive by implying its potential difficulty.

When Liv expressed a renewed desire to "give it a shot," Dana immediately supported this desire, offering encouragement and practical support. This shift repositioned the idea of starting an exercise routine from a challenging commitment to a more achievable goal with support and companionship.

Takeaway Close Approach

Scenario Two

> A manager is trying to encourage an employee to take her entitled vacation days.
>
> *Read the scenario once, then read through it again noting the <u>underlined</u> areas that are most pertinent to the Takeaway Close Approach.*

-ॐॐ-

Manager (Hassan):

Good morning, Jenny.

I noticed you haven't taken any vacation days this year, and I wanted to talk to you about it.

Employee (Jenny):

Hi, Hassan.

Yeah, I've been pretty busy with work, and I didn't want to take time off when there's so much to do.

Hassan:

I understand your dedication Jenny, but it's important to remember that taking time off is also pretty important to maintaining a healthy work-life balance.

Plus, you've accrued quite a few vacation days, and <u>if you don't use them, you might lose them</u>.

Jenny:

Really?

I'd hate to lose any.

But it's just been so hectic lately. I don't want to leave my team in the lurch.

Hassan:

I appreciate your commitment to the team, Jenny.

However, by not taking a break, you could burn out, which wouldn't be beneficial to anyone.

And I know you've probably got some plans outside of work that you've been putting off?

Jenny:

That's true.

I've been wanting to take a trip and spend more time with my family.

Hassan:

Here's what I propose – why don't you plan a vacation next month?

You can use your vacation days, recharge, and come back to work with renewed energy.

We can also ensure that your workload is covered during your absence so that the team won't face any disruptions.

Jenny:

Well, I suppose that makes sense.

A break does sound nice.

Hassan:

Great!

A well-deserved vacation will not only benefit you but also help you come back even more focused and productive.

Plus, you won't have to worry about losing your vacation days.

What do you say?

Jenny:

Alright, Hassan, I'll take your advice.

I'll plan a vacation and make sure everything is in order at work before I go.

-ᡭᢀᡋ-

In this conversation, Hassan used the Takeaway Close Approach to encourage Jenny to use her vacation days and prioritize her well-being. Initially, she was reluctant to take time off, but Hassan told her that not only did she deserve the break, he mentioned the potential loss of unused vacation days. That coupled with the reassurance of covering her workload during her absence made the option of taking a vacation more appealing and achievable.

Takeaway Close Approach

Scenario Three

An employee is in his boss's office presenting a case to secure funding for a new project.

Read the scenario once, then read through it again noting the <u>underlined</u> areas that are most pertinent to the Takeaway Close Approach.

-☙❦-

Employee (Noah):

Hi, Sean.

I wanted to talk to you about the budget allocation for our upcoming project.

It's crucial that we secure the necessary funding to move forward.

Manager (Sean):

Hi, Noah.

I understand the importance of funding, but with the current financial situation, I'm hesitant to make any significant decisions.

Noah:

I get your concerns, Sean.

However, <u>if we don't secure funding for the project soon, we risk losing out on this opportunity</u> altogether.

The resources we're looking at <u>may no longer be available</u>.

Sean:

I see your point, Noah, but it's a tough call.

I'm not sure if we can commit to this right now.

Noah:

I understand your reservations.

It's a big decision, and it comes with its share of risks.

But here's the thing – if we wait too long, we might miss out, and lose the benefits it could bring us.

Other teams are also vying for the same funding.

Sean:

That's true; the competition is fierce.

But what if we secure the funding, and the project doesn't deliver the expected results?

We could be in a difficult position financially.

Noah:

To mitigate the risk, we will work out a comprehensive project plan, outlining clear objectives, milestones, and success criteria.

That way, we'd have a solid roadmap for the project's success and reduce the chances of unexpected setbacks.

Sean:

Having a well-thought-out plan in place would certainly help ease my concerns.

Noah:

I'm glad you think so, Sean.

Let's collaborate on the project plan and ensure we're making an informed decision. If we approach this strategically, I believe the benefits of securing the funding will outweigh the risks.

-❧-

Noah's use of the Takeaway Close Approach to persuade Sean to consider the allocation of the budget for the upcoming project highlighted the urgency and importance of securing the necessary funding, creating a sense of scarcity and potential loss if action wasn't promptly taken.

By mentioning that other teams were also vying for the same funding and that delaying could result in missing out on the opportunity, Noah effectively introduced a sense of competition and urgency.

Now that you're familiar with the **Takeaway Close Approach**, take a few moments to recall a time when you've used or applied the approach and it was helpful in persuading someone to make a decision or motivating them to take action. You may recognize a time and write about when the approach was used to persuade you, as well.

Briefly describe the situation and outcome below.

_____

_____

_____

_____

_____

_____

Next, imagine a situation in the future where you might use this approach in your professional, social, or personal conversations.

_____

_____

_____

_____

_____

_____

_____

"Once a person is determined to help themselves, there is nothing that can stop them."

Nelson Mandela
Politician and Social Activist

The power of self-determination in change is a concept particularly important to persuasive communication. When communicators tap into an individual's goals and values they can personalize and tailor their message into something allied to the listener's personal interests and mission. The interaction between persuasion and self-determination is powerful, and the most enduring and impactful changes occur when people are not just persuaded but become personally committed.

Chapter 10

THE OWNERSHIP CLOSE APPROACH

The Ownership Close Approach is characterized by encouraging the other person to visualize having or experiencing the benefits of the idea or proposal, even before making a commitment. This approach operates on the premise that when someone imagines themselves enjoying the benefits of an idea or proposal, their emotional and psychological attachment to the outcome increases, making them more inclined to proceed.

This approach involves guiding the individual through a vivid, detailed scenario where they are already experiencing the benefits of the offer, creating a sense of ownership, and envisioning themselves on the other side of already having made a decision.

Why it works:

- It enhances perceived value. By allowing the other person to experience the benefits in their mind, you increase the perceived value of the idea or proposal (Kahneman, Knetsch, & Thaler, 1991).
- It stimulates emotional engagement. By encouraging them to visualize owning the offer, this approach engages their emotions, making the decision-making process more personal and compelling.
- It uses the Endowment Effect. Once the other person feels a sense of ownership, even hypothetically, the idea or proposal is valued more highly, a phenomenon known as the Endowment Effect (Thaler, 1980).

The best time to apply it:

- They understand the features of the offer but haven't yet emotionally connected with its value.
- The offer has tangible benefits that can be easily visualized and experienced mentally.
- The interaction is at a stage where building an emotional connection and a sense of ownership can effectively help the decision-making process continue (Kahneman, Knetsch, & Thaler, 1991).

◆◆◆

This approach relies upon imagination, emotional engagement, and the endowment effect to create a sense of ownership, enhancing the perceived value of the idea or proposal, and guides the other person in a positive decision.

Ownership Close Approach

Scenario One

> One teammate wants to encourage the other one to become an even greater athlete.
>
> *Read the scenario once, then read through it again noting the underlined areas that are most pertinent to the Ownership Close Approach.*

-ॐक्ॐ-

Teammate One (Mike):

Lisa, I wanted to chat with you about our upcoming game and your role on the team.

Teammate Two (Lisa):

Sure, what's up, Mike?

Mike:

I've been watching you lately, and I have to say you've got awesome potential.

But I think there's a way for you to take it to the next level and become even better.

Lisa:

Thanks, Mike, that means a lot.

But how do you think I can improve?

121

Mike:

Lisa, I see you as someone who has the potential to be an amazing player and leader.

Picture yourself being known as the teammate who's always giving their best, who never backs down from a challenge.

Visualize yourself as a player who's always there to support and lift up the others, both on and off the field.

Lisa:

That does sound like the kind of player I want to be, but I'm not sure if I have what it takes.

Mike:

Lisa, you absolutely have what it takes.

I believe in you.

Think about it this way – imagine yourself as a leader, making crucial plays and contributing to the team's success.

Picture the respect from your teammates and the respect you'll earn from our competitors.

It's not just about the game…it's about becoming a true champion.

Lisa:

It's kind of inspiring when you put it that way, Mike.

But what steps do you think I should take to get there?

Mike:

It starts with taking responsibility for your development.

Visualize yourself putting in the extra hours at practice, working on your skills, and pushing your limits.

See yourself as someone who is constantly seeking feedback and actively listens to coaches and teammates.

By taking this initiative and continuously working on your game, you can transform yourself into that focused, team-oriented champion you would like to be.

Lisa:

Mike, I really do appreciate your belief in me!

I'm ready to take ownership of my growth.

I can see myself becoming that kind of player.

Mike:

That's the spirit!

I know you have it in you.

With dedication and commitment, you can become a true champion, and we'll all be there to support you every step of the way.

-ॐॐ-

In the conversation, the Ownership Close Approach proved effective in getting Lisa to envision her future and take responsibility for it. Mike painted a vivid picture of Lisa's potential as a champion and emphasized the respect and admiration she would earn, not only boosting her self-esteem but also sparking her innate motivation.

By having Lisa imagine the end result of her hard work, Mike helped Lisa see that the idea of putting in extra effort was both tangible and desirable.

Ownership Close Approach

Scenario Two

A manager wants to help his employee with her workplace self-confidence.

Read the scenario once, then read through it again noting the underlined areas that are most pertinent to the Ownership Close Approach.

-ঙ্কৈ-

Manager (Amir):

Good afternoon, Ella.

I wanted to have a chat with you today.

Employee (Ella):

Hi Amir.

Is there something wrong?

Amir:

Not at all.

In fact, you've done quite well, and I think you're capable of achieving great things here.

But I've sensed that you might not see yourself in the same light.

Ella:

Well, to be honest, I have been struggling a bit lately with my confidence, especially in a professional context.

Pretty dumb, huh?

Amir:

I get it, Ella, and it's not uncommon.

They even have a term for it: Imposter Syndrome.

But I want you to know that your colleagues and I see your strengths and believe in your abilities.

In fact, we've recently introduced some management training programs, and I think you'd be a perfect fit for them.

Ella:

Management training?

I'm not sure if I'm cut out for that.

Amir:

Ella, let me share something with you.

I've seen your dedication and how you've grown in your current role.

These management training programs are designed to help people build confidence and develop leadership skills.

I can most definitely picture you as a successful manager, leading your own team and making a significant impact on our organization.

Ella:

I appreciate your faith in me, but it's hard to imagine myself in that role.

Amir:

I understand that it might seem daunting right now.

But remember, we all start somewhere, and the training will provide you with the tools and knowledge you need to succeed.

I'll provide the opportunities.

[smiles]

Think of it as a journey, with each step bringing you closer to becoming the confident and capable manager I see in you.

Ella:

It's just... I've never really seen myself that way.

You really think I could benefit from the training?

Amir:

Ella, it's totally normal to doubt yourself sometimes, but it's also important to challenge those doubts.

Visualize yourself as a successful manager and leading a team. Think about the satisfaction and pride you'll feel making a difference in that role.

I'll be here supporting you every step of the way, and I believe this is an opportunity for you to take ownership of your professional growth.

Ella:

Okay, Amir, I'll give it a try.

I appreciate your support and belief in me.

Amir:

Alright!

I have no doubt that with determination, this training, and opportunities coming up, you'll surprise yourself and accomplish remarkable things.

We'll work together to help you reach your full potential as a successful manager.

In the scenario, the Ownership Close Approach helped to begin fostering Ella's self-confidence and prompted her to actively consider her professional growth. By painting a clear picture of Ella as a successful manager and outlining a clear path of growth through the training, Amir not only instilled more confidence in Ella but also made the idea of leadership seem more tangible and attainable.

Amir's supportive and envisioning dialogue transformed Ella's doubts into motivation to embrace an opportunity.

Note: When Amir says *"Think about the satisfaction and pride* **you'll** *(you will) feel"* instead of *"Think about the satisfaction and pride* **you'd** *(you would) feel"*, he's introducing a subtle Assumptive Close Approach by phrasing it positively in the future, instead of as a potentiality.

Ownership Close Approach

Scenario Three

In a research laboratory, a lab technician is proposing a new software program to her manager.

Read the scenario once, then read through it again noting the underlined areas that are most pertinent to the Ownership Close Approach.

-ক্ষ্ণ-

Lab Technician (Katey):

Regina, I've been thinking about our workflow and how we could improve it.

Manager (Regina):

I'm always open to suggestions.

What do you have in mind?

Katey:

Well, I've been researching some new productivity software that I believe could really benefit our team.

One of its key features is providing more timely and accurate information, which I think could also make your job easier.

Regina:

Timely and accurate information does sound appealing.

Katey:

Imagine this, Regina.

With this new software, you'd have access to real-time data and reports at your fingertips.

No more waiting for manual updates or dealing with data discrepancies.

You'd be able to make decisions faster and with more confidence, knowing you have the most up-to-date and accurate information.

Regina:

That would be nice.

I'm intrigued, Katey.

So how do you propose we proceed?

Katey:

I suggest we start with a pilot program, involving a small group of team members to get comfortable with the software.

I'll provide training, and we can monitor the results closely.

Once you begin seeing improvements in the information accuracy and speed, we can expand its usage to the whole team.

Regina:

I appreciate your initiative and willingness to lead this effort, Katey.

Let's discuss the details and see how we can move forward with the pilot program.

-❧❧-

Katey engaged Regina's interest in the new productivity software with the Ownership Close Approach by prompting her to envision the tangible benefits it would bring to her role and the team's workflow. Katey presented a scenario where Regina could see the convenience and efficiency of having real-time data and accurate reports and highlighted the direct value to Regina's decision-making process.

By suggesting a pilot program, Katey showed her commitment to lead the initiative and also minimize risk, making the proposal more appealing. Katey's approach generated a willingness in Regina to explore the proposed solution further.

Now that you're familiar with the **Ownership Close Approach**, take a few moments to recall a time when you've used or applied the approach and it was helpful in persuading someone to make a decision or motivating them to take action. You may recognize a time and write about when the approach was used to persuade you, as well.

Briefly describe the situation and outcome below.

_____

_____

_____

_____

_____

_____

_____

Next, imagine a situation in the future where you might use this approach in your professional, social, or personal conversations.

_____

_____

_____

_____

_____

_____

_____

"Great communication begins with connection."

Oprah Winfrey
Media Influencer and Philanthropist

Connection builds trust and openness, and creates a favorable environment for messages to be positively received. By first relating to the audience on a personal or emotional level, communicators can remove barriers and ensure their message not only reaches the audience but resonates with them.

Chapter 11

THE BEN FRANKLIN CLOSE APPROACH

The Ben Franklin Close Approach is named after the famous writer, Statesman, and inventor, who developed it as a decision-making method in 1772. It employs rational analysis and cognitive balance to guide another toward a conclusion. It is employed during conversations where you encourage the other person to list the pros and cons of making a decision. It is also sometimes known as a cost-benefit analysis.

This approach works by guiding the other person through a structured assessment of the advantages and disadvantages associated with the idea or proposal, which enables them to view their decision in a more balanced and comprehensive manner.

Why it works:

- It promotes thoughtful deliberation. By encouraging others to thoroughly analyze their options, it results in a more thoughtful and deliberate decision-making process (Festinger, 1957).
- It reduces cognitive dissonance. By visually arranging the pros and cons, this approach helps them to resolve any cognitive dissonance they might be experiencing (Festinger, 1957).
- It encourages ownership of a decision. This approach reinforces a sense of ownership and personal involvement in the decision-making process when they actively take part in weighing the options (Janis & Mann, 1977).

The best time to apply it:

- They are indecisive or seem overwhelmed by the complexity of the decision.
- There is a clear set of tangible advantages and disadvantages that can be discussed and analyzed.
- They value logical reasoning and appreciate a structured approach to making decisions (Fisher, Ury, & Patton, 2011).

◆◆◆

This approach uses the principles of cognitive balance and thoughtful deliberation. It encourages the other person to critically analyze options and provides a clear structure for them to follow, which enables them to make well-considered decisions.

Ben Franklin Close Approach

Scenario One

> A manager and his employee are discussing the pros and cons of her agreeing to take on a new project.
>
> *Read the scenario once, then read through it again noting the underlined areas that are most pertinent to the Ben Franklin Close Approach.*

-ॐॐ-

Manager (Liam):

Hi, Christina.

I hear you've been contemplating whether or not to take on that project.

What's been holding you back?

Employee (Christina):

Hi, Liam.

I'm concerned about the additional workload and the potential stress it might bring.

Liam;

I understand your apprehension, Christina.

You know that taking on this project will stretch your skills and provide an opportunity for growth.

Christina:

That's true, Liam.

But on the other hand, it could also lead to significantly longer working hours and potentially impact my work-life balance.

Liam:

I appreciate your concerns.

But consider this: by tackling this project, you would gain valuable experience and expertise that might open up new career avenues.

On the flip side, if you decline, you might miss out on a chance for professional development and future opportunities.

Christina:

I am aware of the benefits and consequences.

It's just that I'm worried about the potential burnout.

Liam:

I completely understand your concern about burnout, Christina.

To address that, we can work together on a plan to ensure a manageable workload and provide the support you need throughout the project.

With that in mind, let's take a few minutes to brainstorm the pros and cons of taking on this assignment.

Christina:

[following the brainstorming]

Well, it seems like there's definitely more pros than potential cons.

Now that it's put this way, it sounds pretty reasonable, Liam.

With a well-structured plan in place, I will be more comfortable taking on the challenge.

Liam:

Let's discuss the details and ensure that we can strike a balance between professional growth and your well-being.

Ultimately, this project could be a significant steppingstone in your career.

-ॐॐ-

In the scenario, Liam used the Ben Franklin Close Approach to help Christina carefully consider both sides of a decision to take on a new project. By inviting Christina to openly discuss and collaborate on the pros and cons, Liam was able to emphasize the potential for professional growth and skill enhancement and also address Christina's concerns about workload and work-life balance. His willingness to work with her to develop a structured plan for managing the workload helped to alleviate Christina's apprehensions, shifting her perspective toward the more positive aspects of taking on the role. This approach effectively used a thoughtful decision-making process, where the careful weighing of advantages and disadvantages led to a better understanding of both sides of the situation.

By ensuring that Christina felt supported and her concerns were addressed, the manager was able to guide her toward a decision that aligned with her professional growth and was mindful of her well-being.

Note: Following the brainstorming, the result may have shown more 'cons' than 'pros', in which case Liam could choose to mitigate or reduce any objections or concerns (see Chapter 15) to encourage Christina to take on the role. However, it is the Author's position that accepting a final 'no' as a 'no' is the ethical approach to take, especially when dealing with deeply personal issues.

Ben Franklin Close Approach

Scenario Two

> A husband and wife are discussing the best way to spend their money on their daughter's education.
>
> *Read the scenario once, then read through it again noting the underlined areas that are most pertinent to the Ben Franklin Close Approach.*

-ॐॐ-

Husband (Aaron):

Claire, I've been thinking a lot about our daughter's education lately.

I know a private school would provide a great academic environment, but it comes with a hefty price tag.

Wife (Claire):

Yes, it does.

Private schools are expensive, but saving for college is also crucial.

But think about it this way: if we invested in a private school now, she would receive a first-rate education that might lead to better college opportunities.

Aaron:

True.

I know we both want the best for her future.

But <u>on the other hand</u>, if we saved the money we'd spend on private school and put it toward a college fund, we could potentially provide her with more financial freedom when it's time for higher education.

Claire:

You're right.

College costs are considerable and getting worse, and having a solid fund would alleviate some of the financial burden.

But let's consider the immediate benefits of a private school – smaller class sizes, personalized attention, and a strong academic foundation.

These could really help our daughter's academic journey.

Aaron:

You make a good argument, honey.

It's a tough decision, <u>balancing the immediate benefits of a private school against the long-term financial implications of college</u>.

<u>We should weigh the pros and cons of each carefully, and then compare the two</u>.

Claire:

I agree, Aaron.

<u>Let's take the time to consider our options and make a decision</u> that will provide the best possible future for our child.

-ॐ∽ॐ-

To settle a debate about the issue of deciding between two choices, the couple began using the Ben Franklin Close Approach as they thoughtfully weighed the pros and cons of sending their child to a private school versus saving the money for college. Both parents presented compelling arguments, highlighting the immediate academic and developmental benefits of a private education, against the long-term financial advantages of saving for college, like having more options and avoiding student loans.

Although a final decision has yet to be made, the couple is on the way to figuring out the best way forward. Making the decision to approach the situation and assess the pro's and con's will allow both parties to view it from multiple perspectives, and aid in a balanced and informed decision-making process.

By acknowledging and discussing each other's concerns and the potential outcomes for each choice, the couple will ensure that their decision will be well-considered and aligned with their priorities for their child's education and future financial freedom.

Ben Franklin Close Approach

Scenario Three

> An employee approaches a cautious manager about expanding the company's product line.
>
> *Read the scenario once, then read through it again noting the underlined areas that are most pertinent to the Ben Franklin Close Approach.*

-ॐॐ-

Employee (Paolo):

Steve, I've been thinking about the opportunity to expand our product line, and I believe it could be a game-changer for us.

Manager (Steve):

I've seen the proposal, Paolo, but I'm not entirely convinced it's the right move for us at the moment.

Paolo:

I understand your reservations, but can we take a closer look?

On one hand, if we expand our product line, we could tap into a broader market, potentially increasing our revenue significantly.

Steve:

That's true, but <u>on the other hand</u>, it also comes with added expenses and risks.

141

We'd have to invest in research and development, marketing, and distribution.

Paolo:

All true.

However, if we don't take this opportunity, we might fall behind our competitors who are already exploring similar avenues.

Inaction could lead to stagnation.

Steve:

I see your point, Paolo.

It's just that I'm concerned about the financial aspect.

We need to ensure that the potential gains outweigh the costs.

Paolo:

I completely agree, Steve.

To address that, we can conduct a detailed cost-benefit analysis, estimating the potential returns against the projected expenses.

This way, we'll have a clearer picture of the financial implications.

Steve:

That's a great idea, Paolo.

Having a comprehensive analysis will help us make a more informed decision.

Paolo:

I'm glad you think so, Steve.

With the analysis in place, we can evaluate the potential benefits against the risks, ensuring that we're making a sound and calculated business decision.

-☙❧-

Paolo used the Ben Franklin Close Approach in the scenario to methodically address Steve's hesitations. By acknowledging the potential advantages of market expansion alongside the potential risks and costs, Paolo presented a balanced view of the situation. This approach allowed both parties to openly discuss and recognize the trade-offs involved. Paolo's proposal to conduct a detailed cost-benefit analysis further illustrated the methodical nature of the Ben Franklin Close, which ensured that a decision would not be based on a one-sided perspective but on a comprehensive evaluation of both the positive opportunities and the potential financial implications.

Notice that both Paolo and Steve were interacting using the Ben Franklin Close Approach. In most circumstances, this approach is best used in a collaborative manner.

Now that you're familiar with the **Ben Franklin Close Approach**, take a few moments to recall a time when you've used or applied the approach and it was helpful in persuading someone to make a decision or motivating them to take action. You may recognize a time and write about when the approach was used to persuade you, as well.

Briefly describe the situation and outcome below.

_____

_____

_____

_____

_____

_____

_____

Next, imagine a situation in the future where you might use this approach in your professional, social, or personal conversations.

_____

_____

_____

_____

_____

_____

_____

"Character may almost be called the most effective means of persuasion."

Aristotle
Philosopher

Character and integrity are pivotal in influencing an audience. This principle is central to persuasive communication because when communicators are perceived as ethical, knowledgeable, and empathetic, they gain the trust and respect of their audience. Trust enhances the receptivity of the message, and persuasion becomes easier and more effective. Even more than logic and emotion, the character of the speaker can be the most compelling factor in swaying opinions and inspiring action.

Chapter 12

THE SHARP ANGLE CLOSE APPROACH

The Sharp Angle Close Approach is transactional in nature. Despite its off-putting name, this approach is actually one of the most frequently used of all of the twelve approaches described within this book. This has been called by some the "this for that" approach. It is used when you promptly address and agree to a specific request or condition made by the other person, with the understanding that this concession will lead to some action or commitment by or from them.

This approach operates on the psychological principles underlying decision-making and reciprocity (Kahneman, 2011). It works because it elicits a quick, positive response from the other person by immediately catering to their specific requests or conditions, reducing the time spent in non-essential discussion.

Why it works:

- It engages quick decision-making. When you promptly meet the other person's specific condition, it triggers a rapid decision-making process, leveraging the tendency to make swift decisions when presented with immediate solutions (Kahneman, 2011).
- It creates a reciprocal obligation. This approach employs the Principle of Reciprocity. When you make a concession, the other person is inclined to feel obliged to reciprocate the gesture, increasing the likelihood of a favorable outcome (Goldner, 1960).
- It reduces cognitive load. By providing a clear-cut solution to their situation, you simplify the decision-making process by narrowing down the choices for them, making it easier for them to decide (Schwartz, 2004).

The best time to apply it:

- They have shown genuine interest but are hesitant due to specific concerns or conditions.

- The interaction has reached a mature stage, with them having a complete understanding of the idea or proposal and showing serious consideration for it.
- You can readily meet their conditions without incurring significant inconvenience or cost, ensuring that the concession is a positive compromise (Fisher, Ury, & Patton, 2011).

◆◆◆

This approach is a strategy that facilitates quick decision-making, fosters a sense of obligation through reciprocity, and streamlines the decision-making process by reducing cognitive load.

Sharp Angle Close Approach

Scenario One

A player approaches his Coach about increasing his playing time during his games.

Read the scenario once, then read through it again noting the underlined areas that are most pertinent to the Sharp Angle Close Approach.

-ᗧᗣ-

Player (Kevin):

Coach, I wanted to talk to you about something.

<u>I'd really like to get more playing time on the team.</u>

Coach (Coach Chris):

Hi Kevin, I appreciate your dedication to the team and your desire for more playing time.

It's important to me that every player has an opportunity to play.

What are your thoughts on how we can make that happen?

Kevin:

Well, I've been working really hard on improving my skills, and I've been giving it 100% in practice.

I believe that with more minutes on the field, I can make a bigger impact during games.

Coach Chris:

I've noticed your hard work and dedication, Kevin.

It's clear to me and everyone else that you've been putting in the effort to improve.

Here's the thing – I'm open to giving you more playing time, but I also need to ensure it's in the best interest of the team.

What if we set specific performance goals for you, and once you meet those goals consistently, we can gradually increase your playing time?

Kevin:

That sounds fair, Coach.

I'm up for the challenge, and I'm sure I can meet those goals.

Coach Chris:

Awesome!

Let's set some targets for you and work together to help you achieve them.

Once you consistently meet those goals and demonstrate your impact on the field, I'll have a strong case to increase your playing time.

Kevin:

Thank you, Coach.

I appreciate your helping me on this.

I'm ready to put in the effort and make the most of the opportunity you're giving me.

Coach Chris:

I'm looking forward to seeing your progress, Kevin.

Keep up the hard work, and we'll revisit your playing time as you meet those goals.

-☙❧-

Coach Chris used the Sharp Angle Close Approach to address Kevin's request for more playing time. Instead of denying the request, the coach used a more considered approach by proposing a conditional agreement tied to specific performance goals. This approach shifted the focus from the immediate request for more playing time to a structured plan that incentivized Kevin's continued improvement and commitment. By setting clear performance targets, the coach not only motivated Kevin to further enhance his skills but also aligned Kevin's progress with the overall success of the team.

The Sharp Angle Close Approach in this case proved effective in transforming a straightforward request into a productive and mutually beneficial agreement.

Sharp Angle Close Approach

Scenario Two

> In her office, a manager is discussing an approaching increase in work demands with her employee.
>
> **Read the scenario once, then read through it again noting the <u>underlined</u> areas that are most pertinent to the Sharp Angle Close Approach.**

-ॐॐ-

Manager (Tonya):

Good afternoon, Brian.

I wanted to discuss the upcoming increase in work volume, and how we can manage it effectively.

Employee (Brian):

Hi, Tonya.

As you know, we're already quite busy, and me and my team are already feeling the pressure to meet deadlines with the same quality outputs we've always produced.

Tonya:

I know, Brian.

And I want you to know that I very much appreciate yours and your team's dedication and hard work during the past quarter.

152

Now let me ask you this: <u>given the current workload and future increase, will you be able to handle the additional load and continue to produce the same great work</u>?

Brian:

Honestly, <u>only if we had more hands-on deck and some extra resources to help manage the increased workload.</u>

Tonya:

<u>What if I told you that I'm willing to provide you with the support you need</u>?

We can allocate additional team members to your projects, purchase some new software tools, and even offer some training to enhance productivity.

<u>With these resources, could you commit to taking on the increased workload confidently</u>?

I need to know today.

Brian:

Your suggestion would be a game-changer, Tonya.

With the added support and resources you mentioned, we could probably not only meet but surpass our project deadlines and expectations.

Tonya:

That's great to hear, Brian!

Let's work on a plan to allocate the necessary resources and get you the support you need.

Your commitment and dedication to our projects are truly valuable, and I believe this approach will help both you and the team as a whole.

Brian:

Thank you, Tonya.

I appreciate your willingness to provide the support and resources necessary to tackle the increased workload effectively.

I'm ready to take on the challenge.

-ॐॐ-

In the scenario, Tonya employed the Sharp Angle Close Approach to address the concerns of Brian regarding the pending increase in work demand. Initially, she acknowledged his concerns about the current workload and the pressure his team was facing. When Brian acknowledged that managing the increased workload would be possible with added support, Tonya quickly capitalized on this conditional agreement by offering a direct proposition: providing additional resources in exchange for Brian's commitment to handle the increased workload.

By providing a solution that met Brian's conditions, Tonya showed support and understanding, leading Brian to commit to taking on the new challenge.

Sharp Angle Close Approach

Scenario Three

> An employee and her manager are discussing a new project and role.
>
> *Read the scenario once, then read through it again noting the <u>underlined</u> areas that are most pertinent to the Sharp Angle Close Approach.*

-ॐ৯ॐ-

Manager (Delilah):

Good morning.

I wanted to talk to you about a new project we have coming up.

It's a big one, and I believe you're the right person to take the lead.

Employee (Trish):

Good morning, Delilah.

I appreciate your confidence in me.

I'm definitely interested in learning more about this project.

Delilah:

That's great to hear!

This project involves a significant increase in responsibilities and a higher level of complexity.

I believe you have the skills and dedication to handle it exceptionally well.

This would be a tremendous opportunity and chance to gain some great experience.

Trish:

Thank you for considering me, Delilah.

I'm eager to take on new challenges and deliver great results for the team.

Delilah: I'm happy to hear that.

Trish: With the added responsibilities, would it be reasonable to discuss a pay increase to acknowledge the increased workload?

Delilah:

I understand where you're coming from.

While I'm personally supportive of the idea, we do have budget constraints to consider.

But if we can find a way to adjust your compensation, do you feel confident that you can not only meet but exceed our expectations on this project?

Trish:

Absolutely, Delilah.

I'm confident that with the right resources and support, I can not only meet but excel in this role.

A pay increase would be a motivating factor and a reflection of the value I bring to the team.

Delilah:

Your enthusiasm and commitment are evident, Trish.

Let me discuss this with HR and see what we can do to accommodate your request for a pay increase.

I appreciate your dedication to our projects, and I want to ensure you're rewarded accordingly.

-ॐ᎐᎒-

The Sharp Angle Close Approach was used by Trish as she took the opportunity to begin negotiating a pay increase in response to a new assignment. By linking her request for more compensation to the increased workload and complexity of the project, Trish created a clear and logical connection between her added value and the compensation she sought.

The assertive but respectful approach encouraged the manager to seriously consider her request and commit to discussing it with HR.

Note that Delilah also used the Sharp Angle Close Approach in the conditional agreement to Trish's request to ask for even greater performance.

Now that you're familiar with the **Sharp Angle Close Approach**, take a few moments to recall a time when you've used or applied the approach and it was helpful in persuading someone to make a decision or motivating them to take action. You may recognize a time and write about when the approach was used to persuade you, as well.

Briefly describe the situation and outcome below.

_____

_____

_____

_____

_____

_____

_____

Next, imagine a situation in the future where you might use this approach in your professional, social, or personal conversations.

_____

_____

_____

_____

_____

_____

_____

"Rapport is the ability to enter someone else's world, to make him feel that you understand him, that you have a strong common bond."

Tony Robbins
Motivational Speaker and Author

Rapport is crucial to communicating persuasively because it promotes trust and understanding, makes an audience more open and receptive, and allows for tailored, resonant messaging. The bond reduces resistance, enhances a speaker's influence, and makes the audience more amenable to the message.

Chapter 13

THE PUPPY DOG CLOSE APPROACH

The Puppy Dog Close Approach was named for and evolved from practices in pet sales. Its name and concept are derived from the idea of taking a puppy home for a few days with the expectation that the resulting emotional attachment would lead to a purchase. This strategy gained popularity as a persuasive, low-pressure sales approach, emphasizing product experience over aggressive selling. It capitalizes on the human tendency to form attachments and has been adapted across various industries, from technology to real estate, to enhance customer experience and increase sales success.

For the application of this approach in interpersonal persuasive communication, an individual is offered a temporary, no-strings-attached experience with an idea or proposal, akin to "taking a puppy home for a night." This method is based on the assumption that once the individual discovers the benefits of the idea or proposal, they are likely to make the temporary decision a permanent one.

Why it works:

- It facilitates emotional attachment. By helping the other person to form a bond with an idea or proposal, it increases the likelihood of a permanent, positive decision (Ainslie, 1975).
- It reduces perceived risk. Using a trial period reduces the perceived risk associated with a decision, because the individual feels they have an opportunity to assess the value of the idea or proposal without making a long-term commitment (Kahneman & Tversky, 1979).
- It engages the Principle of Scarcity. Once the other person has experienced benefits, the idea of "going back" to a former state of affairs or losing access makes the offer seem more valuable (Cialdini, 2006).

The best time to apply it:

- The idea's or proposal's value can be best appreciated through direct experience.

- They show or communicate hesitation based on uncertainty about the idea's or proposal's value.
- You aim to build confidence in the idea or proposal by reducing the perceived risk and encouraging firsthand experience (Kahneman & Tversky, 1979).

◆◆◆

This approach uses emotional attachment, risk reduction, and the scarcity principle to encourage a deeper engagement with the idea or proposal, increasing the likelihood of a positive commitment.

Puppy Dog Close Approach

Scenario One

> A wife and her husband are in the kitchen together, while she is making dinner. She desires that her husband share more in the cooking responsibilities.
>
> ***Read the scenario once, then read through it again noting the <u>underlined</u> areas that are most pertinent to the Puppy Dog Close Approach.***

-ঙ্কৎ৯-

Wife (Jessica):

Hey, honey, can we talk about something?

Husband (Michael):

Sure, what's on your mind?

Jessica:

Well, I've been thinking about our meal prep and planning lately, and I was wondering if we could make a little change.

Michael:

What kind of change are you thinking about?

Jessica:

You know how most of the time I'm the one who plans and prepares our meals?

Michael:

Yeah, but you said you enjoyed it!

And I appreciate all the effort you put into it.

Jessica:

Thank you, and most of the time I don't mind at all – I like cooking.

But I'd like us to have a more varied dining experience and share some of the responsibilities a bit more.

I think it would be a great way for us to spend more time together and discover new recipes and flavors.

Michael:

I see where you're coming from, but I'm not exactly a chef in the making.

Cooking really isn't my thing.

Jessica:

I understand, but remember when we went on that trip last summer, and we had that amazing meal at that little local restaurant?

Michael:

Oh yeah, that was fantastic!

The food was incredible.

Jessica:

Well, it got me thinking about how much fun it would be to try new things and explore different cuisines.

And it made me realize that it's not just about the food itself, but also the shared experience of trying something new together.

Michael:

I agree, that was a great memory.

Jessica:

So, <u>what if we could create more of those memories right at home</u>?

And you know what, I believe in you, just like I believed in us when we decided to take that trip.

<u>Imagine what you might create in the kitchen - I think you might surprise yourself</u>!

Michael:

You really think so?

Jessica:

Absolutely!

And <u>to make it easier, we can start small</u>.

I can help you find simple recipes, and we can cook together until you feel comfortable.

<u>If it doesn't work out, we can go back to the old way</u> – and you can make dinner reservations on your nights to cook (laughs).

But I believe that over time, you'll actually enjoy it.

Michael:

Well, when you put it that way, it doesn't sound too intimidating.

I'm willing to try it.

Jessica:

That's great, honey!

I think you'll find it not only enjoyable but also a great way for us to share responsibilities and create a more varied dining experience together.

-☙❧-

In the conversation, Jessica used the Puppy Dog Close Approach to gently persuade her husband to partake in meal planning and preparation by invoking a positive, shared experience (the memorable meal during their trip) to highlight the joy of trying new things together. She then linked that to the idea of cooking together at home. Her approach created an emotional appeal, making the idea of cooking more enticing. She lessened his apprehension by offering support and suggesting a gradual, low-commitment introduction to cooking.

Jessica's strategy effectively reduced the perceived risk and commitment for Michael, which made the proposition more appealing. Her belief in his potential and the prospect of creating enjoyable shared experiences were persuasive, leading her husband to agree to the proposal.

Puppy Dog Close Approach

Scenario Two

> A manager would like her employee to change her work schedule.
>
> *Read the scenario once, then read through it again noting the <u>underlined</u> areas that are most pertinent to the Puppy Dog Close Approach.*

-ↁ·ↂ-

Manager (Sophia):

Thanks for coming in.

I wanted to talk to you about something important today.

Employee (Naomi):

Of course.

What's up, Sophia?

Sophia:

Well, as you know, we've been having some staffing gaps recently, especially during the weekends.

It's been a real challenge for us to ensure proper coverage.

Naomi:

Yeah, I've noticed that too.

It's been quite hectic.

Sophia:

I've been thinking about some solutions to address this issue.

One option that I think will really help us out is if some employees, like yourself, were willing to consider a more flexible schedule.

Naomi:

Flexible schedule?

How would that work?

Sophia:

A flexible schedule would allow you to choose your working hours, within certain guidelines.

You would have more control over your work-life balance.

For example, if you needed to start a bit later or finish earlier on certain days, you could do that.

Naomi:

That does sound appealing, but I'm not sure if it would be possible with my current responsibilities.

Sophia:

I understand and appreciate your concerns, Naomi.

About a year ago, there was a team member who was hesitant about switching to a flexible schedule.

They were worried about balancing their personal life with work.

Naomi:

Really?

What happened?

Sophia:

Well, after some thought, they decided to give it a try.

And you know what happened?

They loved it!

They found that the flexibility allowed them to spend more time with their family and pursue things they were passionate about.

Overall, they were happier and less stressed.

Naomi:

That sounds great, but I'm still not sure how I can make it work.

Sophia:

I don't want you to make any quick decisions.

What I propose is that we give you a trial period, say, for a few weeks.

During that time, we can work together to ensure that the flexible schedule doesn't affect your performance or the team's.

If it doesn't work out, we can always go back to your regular schedule.

Naomi:

That does make it less intimidating.

I suppose I could try it for a few weeks.

Sophia:

That's great, Naomi!

I really appreciate your willingness to consider it.

I believe the flexibility will be a win-win for both you and the team.

And if it works out well, it might become a permanent option for you.

Naomi:

Alright, let's give it a shot, Sophia.

-ॐ&ॐ-

Sophia used the Puppy Dog Close Approach to introduce the idea of a flexible work schedule to Naomi. By presenting the flexible schedule as a low-risk trial with the possibility to revert back, Sophia reduced Naomi's apprehensions and resistance to change. Sophia further strengthened the proposal by sharing a relatable success story of another team member who benefited from such a schedule. The offer to closely monitor and adjust the arrangement during the trial period reassured Naomi that her performance and the team's needs would remain priorities.

Sophia's approach effectively persuaded Naomi to 'test' the new arrangement without feeling locked into a permanent commitment.

Puppy Dog Close Approach

Scenario Three

An employee has a suggestion for his manager concerning the company's employee recognition program.

Read the scenario once, then read through it again noting the <u>underlined</u> areas that are most pertinent to the Puppy Dog Close Approach.

-᎒᎔᎒-

Employee (Youssef):

Hi, Michele, do you have a moment to chat about something?

Manager (Michele):

Of course, Youssef.

What's on your mind?

Youssef:

Well, you know how we have the Employee of the Quarter program that recognizes outstanding individual performance, right?

Michele:

Yes, that's right.

It's a great way to acknowledge the top performers on the team.

Youssef:

Absolutely, but I've been thinking about an idea to increase recognition and morale.

What if we introduced an "Employee of the Quarter for Helping Others Succeed" program, or something named a bit more refined and less wordy?

Michele:

An Employee of the Quarter for helping others?

Hmm…that's an interesting concept.

Can you tell me more about it?

Youssef:

Certainly.

The idea is to recognize employees who go out of their way to support or mentor their colleagues, helping them improve and reach their goals.

It's not about individual achievement but about creating a culture of collaboration and growth within the team.

Michele:

That's a unique approach.

How do you envision it working?

Youssef:

Well, I think we can have a nomination process where team members can recommend their peers who have helped them grow, learn, or overcome challenges.

It could involve mentoring, sharing knowledge, or providing support during tough times.

The winner would receive special recognition and perhaps some extra vacation days as a reward for their efforts.

We can try it for a year, and then assess its effectiveness.

Michele:

I like the idea, Youssef.

It aligns with our company's values of teamwork and personal development.

But how do you think this would impact our existing Employee of the Quarter program?

Youssef:

I don't see it as a replacement, but rather complementary.

<u>The traditional program can continue to acknowledge individual excellence, while this new program would promote a culture of collaboration and support</u>, which benefits everyone in the long run.

Michele:

That makes sense. I appreciate your initiative, Youssef!

It's a refreshing idea that promotes positive team spirit.

Let's discuss this with the HR department and see how we can implement it effectively.

Youssef:

Thank you, Michele.

I really believe this program can help us foster a more supportive and collaborative work environment, and I think it will motivate employees to help each other succeed.

-❧❧-

Youssef used the Puppy Dog Close Approach when proposing his idea by introducing the concept in a non-threatening, appealing manner, emphasizing its potential to enrich the company's culture and team dynamics without immediately asking for a full commitment to the idea. He presented the new program as a complement, not a replacement, to the existing employee recognition system, reducing perceived risks and resistance.

The suggestion to try the program for a year with the option to assess and adjust later significantly lowered the stakes for Michele, encouraging her to consider the proposal's merits without feeling pressured to make a substantial, irreversible decision.

Now that you're familiar with the **Puppy Dog Close Approach**, take a few moments to recall a time when you've used or applied the approach and it was helpful in persuading someone to make a decision or motivating them to take action. You may recognize a time and write about when the approach was used to persuade you, as well.

Briefly describe the situation and outcome below.

_____

_____

_____

_____

_____

_____

_____

Next, imagine a situation in the future where you might use this approach in your professional, social, or personal conversations.

_____

_____

_____

_____

_____

_____

_____

"Excellent communication doesn't just happen naturally. It is a product of process, skill, climate, relationship and hard work."

Pat MacMillan
Author and Chief Executive Officer

Persuasion is not a matter of chance but one of deliberate effort, and awareness of context, capabilities, and relationships. Understanding these and their interplay enables the crafting of messages that resonate more deeply with the audience.

Chapter 14

PUTTING IT ALL TOGETHER

Up to this point, this book has presented, demonstrated, and discussed – individually - twelve different conversational close approaches. Here is a review:

1. Empathy Close Approach: Creates a connection by aligning with and understanding another person.
2. Assumptive Close Approach: Proceeds as if agreement has already been reached following a guided discussion.
3. Alternative Close Approach: Offers choices or options, rather than on whether to continue the discussion or not.
4. Questions Close Approach: Emphasizes open-ended questions to help the other person verbalize their understanding and acceptance of an idea or proposal.
5. Columbo Close Approach: Uncovers reasons for resistance that are unclear or hidden.
6. Similarity Close Approach: Builds and emphasizes connections, establishing common ground or highlighting a shared experience.
7. Being Inoffensive Close Approach: Maintains positive relations throughout the interaction.
8. Takeaway Close Approach: Generates interest or action when an opportunity may be temporary or short-lived.
9. Ownership Close Approach: Imagines or envisions a future situation or set of circumstances.
10. Ben Franklin Close Approach: Compares choices by separating pros and cons.
11. Underline{Sharp Angle Close Approach}: Brings stalled conversations to a close and moves toward a decision.
12. Underline{Puppy Dog Close Approach}: Lets another person try, use, or benefit from something before making a final decision.

In this chapter, you'll be shown over the course of three scenarios how these approaches can be combined into a single conversation. Because of the blending, the conversations will appear more realistic.

All of the conversational approaches from the preceding chapters, and their underlying principles (trust and rapport, empathy and sincerity, ethics and respect) are tools that will help improve how

177

you communicate. They will help make your conversations more effective, whether you're trying to help a friend make a decision, motivate a team member at work, or navigate a discussion about something important with a family member.

They will also help you persuade more effectively in a way that feels - to both parties - natural and genuine. Because it is. Remember that how you talk and your relationship with the other person matters a great deal.

- Focus on encouraging and helping someone see things differently, not manipulate or push them to make a decision.
- Focus on developing and maintaining a positive influence, not on control.
- Focus on supporting, inspiring, and motivating.

As before in preceding chapters, conversational approaches used in each scenario will be pointed out and analyzed. You will see the interplay of the approaches and have an opportunity to look for other approaches not mentioned in the analysis.

You will have an opportunity to identify similarities between approaches. For example, although the Empathy, Being In-offensive, and Similarity Close Approach may seem interchangeable, they are distinctly different, but in some instances any or either of the four may be used, depending upon the context.

◆◆◆

Putting It All Together

Scenario One

This scenario blends the Empathy Close Approach, the Ownership Close Approach, the Alternative Close Approach, and the Assumptive Close Approach.

There may be similarities between these four approaches and others highlighted in this book (demonstrated in Scenarios Two and Three). However, in this Scenario only the approaches listed above will be examined.

-ॐॐ-

A woman wants to persuade her husband to agree to buy new kitchen appliances.

Read through the original dialog, and then read the analyzed dialog that follows with underlined text showing evidence of these approaches.

-ॐॐ-

Wife:

I've been thinking...do you have a minute?

Wouldn't it be great to have a kitchen where we enjoy cooking together more? With newer appliances and a few more bells and whistles, we could experiment with those recipes we've always wanted to try.

Husband:

I like that idea, but I'm thinking about the cost.

Wife:

I agree that it's important we make smart financial decisions.

That's why I looked into it, and there are some energy-efficient models that could save us money in the long run on our utility bills. Plus, think of the quality time we'd spend cooking together in a more efficient kitchen.

Husband:

Okay, I see your point.

Which appliances were you thinking about?"

Wife:

Well, there's the high-tech oven that's perfect for baking and roasting, and the induction cooktop that heats up fast and is super easy to clean.

Both options would be a huge upgrade for us, but I'm leaning towards the oven for its versatility.

What do you think?

Husband:

The oven sounds like a good fit for what we want.

Wife:

Great!

I'll start looking for the best deals for that oven. It'll be exciting to see how it transforms the kitchen and cooking routine.

Husband:

Yeah, I'm looking forward to that.

Let's go for it.

-⌘-

Analyzed Dialog

Wife:

I've been thinking…do you have a minute?

<u>Wouldn't it be great to have a kitchen where we enjoy cooking together more</u> (**Ownership Close Approach**)?

With newer appliances and a few more bells and whistles,<u> we could experiment with those recipes we've always wanted to try</u> (**Ownership Close Approach**).

Husband:

I like that idea, but I'm thinking about the cost.

Wife:

<u>I agree</u> (**Empathy Close Approach**) that it's important we make smart financial decisions.

That's why I looked into it, and <u>there are some energy-efficient models that will save us money in the long run</u> (**Ownership Close Approach**) on our utility bills.

Plus, <u>think of the quality time we'd spend cooking together</u> in a more efficient kitchen (**Ownership Close Approach**).

Husband:

Okay, I see your point.

Which appliances were you thinking about?"

Wife:

Well, <u>there's the high-tech oven</u> that's perfect for baking and roasting with precision, <u>and the induction cooktop</u> that heats up fast and is super easy to clean (both underlined phrases are part of an **Alternative Close Approach**)

<u>Both options</u> (**Alternative Close Approach**) would be a huge upgrade for us, but I'm leaning towards the oven for its versatility.

<u>What do you think</u> (**Empathy Close Approach**)?

Husband:

The oven sounds like a good fit for what we want.

Wife:

Great!

I'll start looking (**Assumptive Close Approach**) for the best deals for that oven.

It'll be exciting to see how it transforms the kitchen and cooking routine.

Husband:

Yeah, I'm looking forward to that.

Let's go for it.

-ॐ∞-

The scenario effectively blended four approaches, enabling a persuasive and non-manipulative conversation leading to a positive outcome.

The **Ownership Close Approaches** immediately set a positive tone for the conversation, encouraging the husband to imagine the benefits and the enhanced experiences they would have with new appliances. Later, the approach was used to help address questions. Each use of the approach helped to increase the emotional investment in the outcome.

The **Empathy Close Approaches** showed understanding and addressed the husband's concerns about cost, and it created an opportunity to highlight the long-term savings and emotional benefits, which makes the proposition more appealing. By asking her husband for his thoughts, the wife further built rapport during the conversation.

The **Alternative Close Approaches** presented specific options for upgrading the kitchen, giving the husband a sense of control and involvement in the decision-making process. This effectively narrowed the conversation from whether to upgrade to which appliance to choose, moving towards the purchase decision.

Finally, the **Assumptive Close Approach** assumed the purchase was a foregone conclusion, focusing on the positive impact the new oven will have. This approach used the momentum built up during the conversation and guided it toward taking action without blatantly asking for agreement. Note that this approach, although not the last in the scenario, was the one used to move the husband forward.

Together, these approaches were able to create an emotional appeal, practical considerations, and a shared vision, making the decision to purchase a natural and mutual choice.

-〜〜-

Other approaches were also present in this scenario, though not pointed out or analyzed:

- Being Inoffensive Close Approach
- Questions Close Approach

Did you find where they were used? Did you notice any approaches that could have been substituted with another?

◆◆◆

Putting It All Together

Scenario Two

This scenario blends the Similarity Close Approach, the Questions Close Approach, the Puppy Dog Close Approach, and the Columbo Close Approach.

There may be similarities between these four approaches and others highlighted in this book (demonstrated in Scenarios One and Three). However, in this Scenario only the approaches listed above will be examined.

-ॐॐ-

Two friends are having a conversation. One friend, who does yoga, wants to persuade her friend to try yoga, too.

Read through the original dialog, and then read the analyzed dialog that follows with underlined text showing evidence of these approaches.

-ॐॐ-

Maria:

I've been thinking about how stressed we've been with work lately. Doing yoga has been my lifesaver.

I feel like it could really help you too since we're both dealing with the same kind of stress.

Nina:

I've seen how much you enjoy it, but I'm not sure it's for me. I'm not very flexible.

184

Maria:

I understand where you're coming from. I was the same way at first.

But let me ask you, what if you could try a class where everyone is a beginner, and it's all about personal growth, not competition?

Would you feel more comfortable giving it a shot then?

Nina:

That does sound a bit more appealing. Maybe I will try it in the future.

Maria:

Why wait?

The studio is doing a free introductory class this weekend. It's super relaxed, and I can come with you if you'd like. You don't have to commit to anything beyond that.

It's just like when we tried that new cafe downtown - no strings attached.

Nina:

Thanks, but I need to think about it.

[They continue chatting about other things, moving off the topic of yoga.]

Maria:

Going back to the yoga thing, you mentioned wanting to find activities that help with relaxation and focus, right?

Imagine finding out that yoga is exactly what you've been looking for. What if this one class is the key to unlocking a new passion or a way to unwind?

What's holding you back?

Nina: [laughing] I just don't want to look stupid and awkward, I guess.

But you know, because you're coming with me, I think I'll give it a try. Thanks for keeping me focused.

Maria:

I've been thinking about how stressed we've been (**Similarity Close Approach**) with work lately.

Doing yoga has been my lifesaver.

I feel like it could really help you too since we're both dealing with the same kind of stress (**Similarity Close Approach**).

Nina:

I've seen how much you enjoy it, but I'm not sure it's for me.

I'm not very flexible.

Maria:

I understand where you're coming from (**Similarity Close Approach**).

I was the same way (**Similarity Close Approach**) at first.

But let me ask you, what if you could try a class where everyone is a beginner (**Questions Close Approach**), and it's all about personal growth, not competition?

Would you feel more comfortable (**Questions Close Approach**) giving it a shot then?

Nina:

That does sound a bit more appealing.

Maybe I will try it in the future.

Maria:

Why wait (**Questions Close Approach**)?

The studio is doing a free introductory class this weekend (**Puppy Dog Close Approach**).

It's super relaxed, and I can come with you if you'd like.

You don't have to commit (**Puppy Dog Close Approach**) to anything beyond that.

It's just like when we tried that new cafe downtown - <u>no strings attached</u> (**Puppy Dog Close Approach**).

Nina:

Thanks, but I need to think about it.

[They continue chatting about other things, moving off the topic of yoga.]

Maria:

<u>Going back to the yoga thing, you mentioned wanting to find activities that help with relaxation and focus, right</u> (**Columbo Close Approach**, after Nina thinks the conversation has moved on)?

Imagine finding out that yoga is exactly what you've been looking for.

What if this one class is the key to unlocking a new passion or a way to unwind?

<u>What's holding you back</u> (**Questions Close Approach**)?

Nina: I just don't want to look stupid and awkward, I guess.

[laughs]

But you know, because you're coming with me, I think I'll give it a try.

Thanks for keeping me focused.

-ᘓᘗ-

The conversation skillfully integrated four approaches, culminating in the friend agreeing to try yoga.

The **Similarity Close Approaches** established common ground between the friends and maintained rapport, with Maria making the suggestion to try yoga not just because she enjoyed it but as solution to a mutual problem. This fostered a sense of camaraderie and trust.

The **Questions Close Approaches** engaged Nina directly, making her part of the decision-making process and addressed her concerns in a hypothetical and reassuring scenario. This made the possibility of trying yoga feel safer and tailored to Nina.

The **Puppy Dog Close Approaches** included mentioning the no-risk trial, likening the yoga class to a casual, try-it-and-see experience. This effectively lowered the barrier to trying it by removing the fear of commitment and emphasizing the temporary nature of the trial.

The deliberate use of the **Columbo Close Approach** after the conversation appeared to have moved on served as an effective and thoughtful nudge. It allowed Maria a chance to discover the "real reason" for the hesitation, reconnected the opportunity to try yoga with Nina's expressed desires for relaxation and focus and presented the trial class as a potential solution to her broader goals. This less direct, reflective question encouraged Nina to reconsider her hesitance and framed the decision to try yoga in a new, more positive light. Note that this approach, although not the last in the scenario, was the one used to move Nina forward.

Together, these techniques created a persuasive narrative that was both empathetic and strategic, leading Nina to decide to try yoga with an open mind and a sense of curiosity, rather than feeling pressured or overwhelmed.

-ॐ-

Another approach was also present in this scenario, though not pointed out or analyzed:

- Ownership Close Approach

Did you find where it was used? Did you notice any approaches that could have been substituted with another?

◆◆◆

Putting It All Together

Scenario Three

-ॐॐ-

This scenario blends the Being Inoffensive Close Approach, the Ben Franklin Close Approach, the Takeaway Close Approach, and the Sharp Angle Close Approach.

There may be similarities between these four approaches and others highlighted in this book (demonstrated in Scenarios One and Two). However, in this Scenario only the approaches listed above will be examined.

-ॐॐ-

Two parents are encouraging their son, who is anxious about his future and is procrastinating, to make a decision soon about where to go to college.

Read through the original dialog, and then read the analyzed dialog that follows with underlined text showing evidence of these approaches.

-ॐॐ-

Mom:

We've noticed you've been a bit hesitant about choosing a college, and we completely understand. It's a big decision, and it's okay to feel anxious about it.

We're here to support you, no matter what.

Son:

Yeah, I just can't seem to decide.

189

Every option seems to have its pros and cons, and I'm worried I'll make the wrong choice.

Dad:

It's natural to weigh the pros and cons. What if we list them out together?

For example, College A has a great program for your major, but it's farther from home. College B is closer, but the program isn't as strong.

Laying it all out like this could help you make your decision.

Son:

I suppose that could help, but I still feel stuck.

Mom:

What if we look at this differently?

If the decision is too overwhelming right now, perhaps we could consider deferring enrollment for a year. This way, you don't feel pressured into making a hasty decision.

Son:

I hadn't thought about deferring. I don't really want to delay starting college, though.

Dad:

We understand. Whatever decision you make, we'll support it.

But if you were to make a decision by tomorrow, we could start planning the next steps together, whether it's visiting the campus again or looking into housing.

How does that sound?

Son:

You know, that actually makes a lot of sense. I think I can do that.

I'll sleep on it and make my decision by tomorrow.

-❧-

Mom:

We've noticed you've been a bit hesitant about choosing a college, and <u>we completely understand</u> (**Being Inoffensive Close Approach**).

It's a big decision, and it's okay to feel anxious about it.

<u>We're here to support you, no matter what</u> (**Being Inoffensive Close Approach**).

Son:

Yeah, I just can't seem to decide.

Every option seems to have its pros and cons, and I'm worried I'll make the wrong choice.

Dad:

It's natural to <u>weigh the pros and cons</u> (**Ben Franklin Close Approach**).

What if we list them out together?

For example, College A has a great program for your major, but it's farther from home.

College B is closer, but the program isn't as strong.

<u>Laying it all out like this</u> (**Ben Franklin Close Approach**) could help you make your decision.

Son:

I suppose that could help, but I still feel stuck.

Mom:

What if we look at this differently?

If the decision is too overwhelming right now, <u>perhaps we could consider deferring enrollment for a year</u> (**Takeaway Close Approach**).

<u>This way, you don't feel pressured into making a hasty decision</u> (**Takeaway Close Approach**).

Son:

I hadn't thought about deferring.

I don't really want to delay starting college, though.

Dad:

We understand.

Whatever decision you make, we'll support it (**Being Inoffensive Close Approach**).

But if you were to make a decision by tomorrow, we could start planning the next steps together (**Sharp Angle Close Approach**), whether it's visiting the campus again or looking into housing.

How does that sound?

Son:

You know, that actually makes a lot of sense.

I think I can do that.

I'll sleep on it and make my decision by tomorrow.

-❧❧-

The conversation effectively combined four approaches in a parental context to guide their son towards making a college decision.

The **Being Inoffensive Close Approaches** set up a supportive and understanding environment, making it easier for the son to open up about his anxiety without feeling judged. This approach reassured him that his feelings were valid and that he had his parents' unconditional support, which is crucial for someone struggling with anxiety and indecision.

The **Ben Franklin Close Approaches** provided a logical framework for decision-making, encouraging the son to methodically evaluate his options. This technique helped to break down the overwhelming decision into manageable parts, making the process seem less daunting.

The **Takeaway Close Approaches** subtly shifted the pressure away from making the perfect choice right now by presenting the option to defer. This "reverse psychology" use of the approach made the original decision of choosing a college more appealing than the alternative of delaying his education.

Lastly, the **Sharp Angle Close Approaches** used the son's reluctance to defer as a motivational tool. By suggesting a specific timeframe for the decision, it created a sense of timeliness and clarity, prompting action where there was previously hesitation. Note that this approach was the one used to motivate the son to not delay his decision.

Together, these techniques worked by balancing emotional support with logical decision-making strategies, effectively nudging the son towards committing to a decision in a way that felt self-motivated and supported, rather than pressured.

-☙❧-

Other approaches were also present in this scenario, though not pointed out or analyzed:

- Empathy Close Approach
- Similarity Close Approach.

Did you find where they were used? Did you notice any approaches that could have been substituted with another?

◆◆◆

This chapter provided some examples of how you can use and blend several conversational approaches in regular conversations to help others, make connections stronger, and get people to take action.

Practical applications of combined conversation approaches across three scenarios demonstrated natural, empathetic, and effective use, and provided a deeper understanding of how to communicate persuasively and positively in everyday conversations.

Keep in mind that context and the relational dynamics between those engaged in a conversation are particularly important - they will shape the choice of which approaches are most relevant and appropriate to use and blend together.

If it were **_you_** participating in the scenario conversations, would you have substituted an approach or changed the order of presentation?

By understanding and using these conversational approaches wisely, you will become better at persuading and motivating the people around you in a positive and respectful way.

Chapter 15

RESPONDING TO OBJECTIONS
AND CONCERNS

Objections and concerns are normal, should be expected, and should be welcomed! Why? Because when someone lets you know there's a concern, worry, or issue with what you're proposing, it means that they care enough to continue the discussion and are interested in what you have to say, offer, or do.

Objections and concerns often arise during conversations when an individual is prompted to make a decision or take some form of action due to a natural resistance to change and an instinct to avoid risk (or the unknown). Most people prefer to maintain their status quo, which includes their beliefs and understanding. People tend to prefer avoiding losses over acquiring equivalent gains, which makes the idea of change even less appealing to them (Cialdini, 2006). And more often than not objections can stem from a lack of information about or a misunderstanding around your intended message.

When individuals don't have (or believe they don't have) all the facts, when they understand the information differently than you expected, or perceive your information from a different or novel viewpoint, they are very likely to object or raise a concern as a way to seek clarity and reassurance before stepping out of their comfort zone. Objections can and often do reveal an individual's unique set of values, beliefs, and past experiences. When a proposed change conflicts with these personal elements, resistance is natural because individuals seek to protect them.

There are quite a few methods that have been developed that work to ensure people with objections feel respected, heard, and understood. These give you the opportunity to answer questions and concerns and move forward with what you're trying to accomplish or get across. Some methods even use actual scripts - don't use those. Within the context of this book (which focuses on interpersonal communication and persuasion – not sales or customer service), they can be seen as disingenuous and insincere. As our colleagues, friends, and family become more sophisticated and savvier, scripts will invariably backfire. One size *doesn't* fit all.

The steps used in responding to objections range in number from four to as many as a dozen; what's important to note is that regardless of the number of steps, they all essentially contain the same elements, often blended together. And, generally speaking, as long as all the elements are addressed, the order can (and should) be fluid to allow it to follow the course of a normal conversation.

In this book, I'm presenting a six-step model that includes those elements, which can be remembered by the acronym ACERAC: Acknowledge, Clarify, Empathize, Restate, Address, Confirm.

1. Acknowledge

Acknowledging a person's objection or concern means first and foremost that you have paid attention and noted either a stated concern or question, or an implied one. Avoid defensiveness or becoming patronizing. An example of acknowledging a concern might be "you seem concerned about the new schedule."

In some cases, an individual may not even be aware of their tone or body language. By asking more general questions, such as "you seem to have a question" or "I noticed you seemed thoughtful about something I just said," you're letting the individual know you're paying attention to them.

2. Clarify

This is one of the most challenging elements in overcoming objections - discovering what the real and complete objection or concern is. This happens by asking questions. When you do not, you may end up with the wrong issue, perception, or interpretation.

For example, imagine a salary negotiation between a corporate recruiter and a job applicant who has asked for $1,000 more for a position, which exceeds what the recruiter can offer.

What if the recruiter asks conversationally about what the additional $1,000 was for? The applicant mentions that they need the added income to help complete their college degree and undertake some professional certification courses to further their career.

The true objection/concern in this case is not the need for $1,000 extra dollars, but about not feeling they will have enough money to complete their degree.

3. Empathize

Empathizing does not mean agreement. It means that you value the other person's perspective and recognize that their objection or concern is valid to them. Expressing empathy requires a combination of attention, active listening, and humility.

You must be alert to tone and non-verbal clues and try to understand their emotions. Seek to expand the conversation by asking open-ended questions to get more in-depth answers. Mirroring the individual's word choices, body language, and tone can reinforce that their message to you is being received and understood.

4. Restate

In this step, paraphrase in your own words what you heard them tell you about the objection or concern. "So, it seems that _____, is that correct?" is an example of restating.

In the event you haven't gotten it quite right, are wrong, or the individual wasn't clear enough, this is where you have the opportunity to dialog back and forth until you have the situation correctly and to the satisfaction of the other person.

In your own personal or professional life, have you ever tried to solve the wrong interpersonal problem? At best, it's usually a time waster and distraction; at worst, it can aggravate the other person and damage rapport and even relationships.

Don't move on in this process until you are <u>both</u> satisfied you understand the situation.

Ensuring you've noticed a question or concern, have refined it down to its main points, established and maintained rapport with the individual, and let the individual know you're about to address their situation, you are now ready to move forward with addressing it.

5. Address

Essentially, objections can be grouped into two categories: *confusion* and *obstacles*. Each requires a different approach.

When an individual is confused or seems to have a misunderstanding, resolve the issue by a reclarification of what you had discussed earlier, in a slightly different manner (but be alert to the fact that the information must be consistent to what was earlier presented) and by engaging in more dialog with the individual. Sometimes, confusion or misunderstandings are simply due to a lack of information.

To go back to our earlier recruiter/applicant example, the recruiter might choose to remind [re-*clarify*] the applicant about the company's annual $2,500 tuition reimbursement as well as partnerships with several technical certification institutions that provide free training to employees. By addressing the concern, the recruiter can show the applicant that they would have the ability to complete a college degree with the company providing more money toward their education and training, than receiving an additional $1,000 annually.

The recruiter cleared up a misunderstanding and provided more detailed information.

Obstacles are a bit more challenging, and often are a result of not being able to meet a request, need, or condition. One of the best ways to overcome this type of objection or concern is to use a combination of context, trust and rapport, and approach it with an attitude of compromise; in fact, using one or a combination of the twelve approaches provided in this book are invaluable in overcoming obstacles.

For example, a mother and her teenage daughter are having a spirited conversation about a perceived overly restrictive curfew. Both understand and respect each other's opinion and position, and why they have them.

Following a heart-to-heart conversation, a compromise is reached: on weekdays the regular curfew of 10 pm remains, and on weekends the daughter may stay out until midnight but must text when she arrives at a friend's house and when she leaves.

6. Confirm

Ensure that your responses addressing the concerns are understood and accepted, and then ask if they were adequately addressed.

What happens if the answer is "no?" Remember that you're still communicating, which means the individual is still interested in what you're saying or trying to do, and wants more clarity, information or closure – otherwise, they would end the discussion or meeting either directly and explicitly or by agreeing solely for the sake of ending the conversation.

If the objection hasn't been overcome or the concern suitably addressed, ask more questions, make sure you accurately understand the real objection or concern, and provide clear, relevant information to address any remaining confusion and acceptable and realistic solutions to obstacles.

◆ ◆ ◆

Will you satisfy all objections and concerns every time? No, and that's okay. Sometimes the objections and concerns have merit due to information you don't have or don't know about. And ethically, morally, and for the sake of maintaining positive relationships, sometimes it may be best to just let it go, and possibly revisit the issue or proposal at a later date.

-ॐॐ-

Example Conversation Using ACERAC
to Overcome an Objection

Wife (**Heather**):

I'm not sure about moving to this new house. It's so far from my workplace and the kids' school.

Husband (**Jason**):

(**Acknowledge**) I hear you saying that the distance is a concern. Is there anything else about the move that's bothering you?

Heather:

Well, yes. I'm also worried about the cost of living there. It seems like everything will be more expensive.

Jason:

(**Clarify**) Hmm, so I'm hearing that the big issues are the distance and the cost of living.

(**Empathize**) I can understand why those things would worry you. Being further away from your job and the kids' school could make your daily routine more difficult, and higher living costs are definitely a concern.

(**Restate**) So to make sure I've got this right: You're worried that the new house is too far from your work and the kids' school, and you're also concerned about the potential increase in our living expenses. Did I get that right?

Heather:

Yes, that's exactly it.

Jason:

Okay, I totally get where you're coming from.

(**Address**) I want you to know that I did some homework, and I've learned that there are good public transport options that might actually make your commute easier than it is now. Plus, the new house is closer to a better school for the kids. As for the cost of living, it's true that some things are a bit more expensive, but the new house is more energy-efficient, which will save us money on utilities. And the neighborhood has amenities that will save us money in other ways, like a community garden and free events for families.

Heather:

I hadn't thought about the savings from energy efficiency and the local amenities. That does help balance things out a bit.

Jason:

(**Continue to Address**) So, with the easier commute for you and better school for the kids, along with savings from the energy-efficient home and local amenities, do you feel a bit more comfortable with the idea of moving?

Heather:

Yes, I do. I think I just needed to talk through it all. I appreciate you taking the time to address my concerns.

Jason:

Of course! I want to make sure we're both happy with the decision.

(**Confirm***)* <u>So, do you think you're ready to start planning the move, or is there anything else you'd like to discuss</u>?

-ॐॐ-

In this dialogue, Jason effectively goes through the objection handling process by recognizing and identifying the objections (distance and cost). He then acknowledged and empathized with Heather's concerns, clarifying and restating her objections to show his understanding. He attended to the objections proactively by providing information on public transport, school quality, and cost savings, again confirming understanding, and finally, checked to see if the objections have been addressed by asking if Heather was ready to begin planning the move.

◆ ◆ ◆

To summarize this Chapter, remember that objections and concerns are good things to have in a persuasive discussion; it means that you are making progress! Although there are many systems and methods for overcoming objections, as long as the core elements are present and achieved, regardless of the order or emphasis (which may ebb and flow within a conversation), you are likely to move forward and be successful.

Chapter 15

THREE IMPORTANT EXPRESSIONS

All the preceding approaches in this book rely upon your ability to establish and nurture rapport, trust, and adopt an attitude and willingness to influence another person in a positive direction. These approaches are nothing more than tools to help you do so. Often, the result will be a positive outcome for both of you. To move someone toward a greater and deeper consideration, or to motivate someone to take action that is in their best interest is a cornerstone and key skill of leadership, friendship, partnering and parenting.

In closing this book, I'd like to leave you with three important expressions. Think of them not as additional elements to the approaches in this book, but rather as something to keep in mind and frequently use when interacting with others.

please

thank you

because

These words are important in that they esteem and acknowledge the value of the one you're speaking to in a conversation.

Even in cases where there is a significant professional, social, or relationship gap (e.g., parent-young child), and agreement or compliance is expected or required, *please* is a word that will go a long way in showing respect for the other person.

Thank you is important when it is deserved and earned, and makes the person feel seen, valued, and appreciated.

Because explains the "why," and shows that you regard the one spoken to enough to explain or present a rationale, rather than simply asking for something or requiring compliance. It will also often yield greater results and outcomes due to the context you provide and is helpful to you because it encourages dialog and feedback to help you make the "ask" more refined, complete, or accurate.

These three expressions cost you nothing and positively influence others (not to mention being courteous). Few, if any, people you encounter in your professional, social, or familial circles will object to their use, so use them when opportunities arise - you never know when a kind and well-placed word will make all the difference to someone.

"To laugh often and much; to win the respect of intelligent people and the affection of children...to leave the world a better place...to know even one life has breathed easier because you have lived. This is to have succeeded."

Ralph Waldo Emerson
Philosopher and Essayist

AFTERWORD

What you say and do will matter to people that you may never meet.

The way we engage with others leaves a lasting impression. How we communicate has a domino effect and touches other people and events far from where our words are spoken. How we interact with others – not only our words and delivery but the motivation behind them - impacts how they, in turn, will interact with others.

From our earliest communications to our most mature interactions in personal and professional situations, the art of persuasion is a fundamental skill we all have and continuously refine throughout our lives. Our skill as a persuader is shaped and sharpened through observation and participating in countless conversations, learning from successes and failures when trying to persuade others - and from experiencing attempts from others to persuade us.

This book highlighted the twelve most-used closing approaches that are used in routine, everyday interactions. These approaches facilitate effective persuasion by improving understanding and furthering agreement in a respectful and non-coercive manner. Foundational to all twelve of these approaches are trust and rapport, both of which require time and a genuine effort to cultivate. Empathy, sincerity of communication, ethics and a respect for the individuality and autonomy of others are also fundamental.

Persuasion in daily interactions relies on building and maintaining trust and understanding and fostering relationships that become stronger rather than strained. The difference between persuasion and manipulation is an important one - ***persuasion*** operates from a place of respect, integrity, and a sincere desire to help the other person using positive influence.

REFERENCES

Ainslie, G. (1975). Specious reward: A behavioral theory of impulsiveness and impulse control. Psychological Bulletin, 82(4), 463-496.

Cialdini, R. B. (2006). Influence: The Psychology of Persuasion. Harper Business.

Deci, Edward L.; Ryan, Richard M. (1985). Intrinsic motivation and self-determination in human behavior. New York: Plenum.

Festinger, L. (1957). A Theory of Cognitive Dissonance. Stanford, CA: Stanford University Press.

Fisher, R., Ury, W., & Patton, B. (2011). Getting to Yes: Negotiating Agreement Without Giving In. New York, NY: Penguin Books.

Goldner, A.W. (1960). The Norm of Reciprocity: A Preliminary Statement. American Sociological Review, 25(2), 161-178.

Janis, I. L., & Mann, L. (1977). Decision-making: A psychological analysis of conflict, choice, and commitment. Free Press.

Kahneman, D. (2011). Thinking, Fast and Slow. New York, NY: Farrar, Straus and Giroux.

Kahneman, D., & Tversky, A. (1979). Prospect Theory: An Analysis of Decision under Risk. Econometrica.

Kahneman, D., Knetsch, J. L., & Thaler, R. H. (1991). Anomalies: The Endowment Effect, Loss Aversion, and Status Quo Bias. The Journal of Economic Perspectives, 5(1), 193-206.

Mayer, J. D., DiPaolo, M., & Salovey, P. (1990). Perceiving affective content in ambiguous visual stimuli: A component of emotional intelligence. Journal of Personality Assessment, 54(3-4), 772-781.

Monroe, K. B. (2003). Pricing: Making Profitable Decisions. New York, NY: McGraw-Hill.

Paul, R., & Elder, L. (2006). The Miniature Guide to Critical Thinking Concepts and Tools. Dillon Beach, CA: Foundation for Critical Thinking.

Rogers, C. R. (1951). Client-centered therapy: Its current practice, implications, and theory. Boston: Houghton Mifflin.

Rogers, C. R. (1961). On Becoming a Person: A Therapist's View of Psychotherapy. London: Constable.

Rogers, E. M. (2003). Diffusion of Innovations. Free Press.

Schein, E. H. (2013). Humble Inquiry: The Gentle Art of Asking Instead of Telling. San Francisco, CA: Berrett-Koehler Publishers.

Schwartz, B. (2004). The Paradox of Choice: Why More Is Less. New York, NY: Ecco.

Thaler, R. (1980). Toward a positive theory of consumer choice. Journal of Economic Behavior & Organization, 1(1), 39-60.

Tversky, A., & Kahneman, D. (1981). The Framing of Decisions and the Psychology of Choice. Science, 211(4481), 453-458.

Tversky, A., & Kahneman, D. (1991). Loss Aversion in Riskless Choice: A Reference-Dependent Model. The Quarterly Journal of Economics, 106(4), 1039-1061.

ABOUT THE AUTHOR

Dr. Benson has worked with dozens of organizations within the corporate, government, military, and entrepreneurial domains for over four decades. A skilled advisor and influential leader, he has experience creating and guiding organizational development initiatives, forging strategic partnerships, recruiting, educating, and mentoring. Dr. Benson has a passion for increasing the capabilities of organizations through the development of individuals.

The author holds a Doctorate in Organizational Leadership and a Master of Arts in Adult Education. The author is certified as both a Senior Professional in Human Resources by the Human Resources Certification Institute and a Senior Certified Professional in Human Resources by the Society for Human Resources Management. Additional certifications include E-Learning Instructional Designer from the Association for Talent Development and MBTI® Certified Practitioner from the Myers & Briggs Foundation.

The author currently lives in the Washington, D.C. area.

www.ingramcontent.com/pod-product-compliance
Lightning Source LLC
Chambersburg PA
CBHW060450280326
41933CB00014B/2721